Bank of England and Financial Services Act 2016

CHAPTER 14

Explanatory Notes are available separately

GRAN*GIS* UK Publishing

Adapted and published by GRANGIS (Grand Register Library).
Online: www.grangis.com
E-mail: contact@grangis.com

In this version:
ISBN: 979-8-88559-006-8

Note: This is the original version (as it was originally enacted). Title, sub-title and the generated date is as marked on the pages.

Bank of England and Financial Services Act 2016

CHAPTER 14

BANK OF ENGLAND AND FINANCIAL SERVICES ACT 2016

PART 1

THE BANK OF ENGLAND

Governance

Financial arrangements

Prudential regulation

Bank of England and Financial Services Act 2016

2016 CHAPTER 14

An Act to make provision about the Bank of England; to make provision about the regulation of financial services; to make provision about the issue of banknotes; and for connected purposes. [4th May 2016]

BE IT ENACTED by the Queen's most Excellent Majesty, by and with the advice and consent of the Lords Spiritual and Temporal, and Commons, in this present Parliament assembled, and by the authority of the same, as follows:—

PART 1

THE BANK OF ENGLAND

Governance

1 Membership of court of directors

(1) The Bank of England Act 1998 is amended as follows.

(2) In section 1(2) (court of directors) after paragraph (b) insert—

"(ba) a Deputy Governor for markets and banking,".

(3) After section 1 insert—

"1A Power to alter membership of court of directors

(1) The Treasury, after consulting the Governor of the Bank, may by order amend the list in section 1(2) so as to—

(a) alter the title of a Deputy Governor;

(b) add a Deputy Governor to the list;

(c) remove a Deputy Governor from the list.

(2) An order under subsection (1)(a) or (c) must (by making saving provision or otherwise) secure that the alteration in the title of a Deputy Governor or the removal of a Deputy Governor from the list in section 1(2) does not have effect in relation to the individual (if any) who holds that office at the time the order is made.

(3) An order under subsection (1)(b) may also add the Deputy Governor to which the order relates to the list in—

(a) section 9B(1) (membership of Financial Policy Committee);

(b) section 13(2) (membership of Monetary Policy Committee);

(c) section 30A(2) (membership of Prudential Regulation Committee).

(4) An order under subsection (1)(c) may also remove from any of those lists the Deputy Governor to which the order relates.

(5) Where an order under subsection (1) makes an amendment mentioned in column 1 of the following table, it may also make the amendment mentioned in the corresponding entry in column 2 of the table.

Addition or removal of Deputy Governors	*Corresponding change in membership of Committee*
Addition of one or more Deputy Governors to the list in section 9B(1)	Equal increase in the number of members appointed by the Chancellor of the Exchequer under section 9B(1)(e)
Removal of one or more Deputy Governors from the list in section 9B(1)	Equal reduction in the number of members appointed by the Chancellor of the Exchequer under section 9B(1)(e)
Addition of one or more Deputy Governors to the list in section 13(2)	Equal reduction in the number of members appointed by the Governor of the Bank under section 13(2)(b)
Removal of one or more Deputy Governors from the list in section 13(2)	Equal increase in the number of members appointed by the Governor of the Bank under section 13(2)(b)
Addition of one or more Deputy Governors to the list in section 30A(2)	Equal increase in the minimum number of members appointed by the Chancellor of the Exchequer under section 30A(2)(g)
Removal of one or more Deputy Governors from the list in section 30A(2)	Equal reduction in the minimum number of members appointed by the Chancellor of the Exchequer under section 30A(2)(g)

(6) The power in subsection (5)—

(a) to make an equal reduction in the number of members appointed under section 9B(1)(e), 13(2)(b) or 30A(2)(g), includes power to remove the power to make those appointments where an equal reduction would reduce the number of members so appointed to zero,

(b) to make an equal increase in the number of members appointed under section 9B(1)(e), 13(2)(b) or 30A(2)(g), includes power to reinstate the power to make those appointments where it has previously been removed under paragraph (a).

(7) An order under subsection (1) may amend, repeal or revoke any provision made by or under any Act, including this Act, so as to make consequential provision."

2 Term of office of non-executive directors

(1) Paragraph 2 of Schedule 1 to the Bank of England Act 1998 (term of office of non-executive directors) is amended as follows.

(2) The existing text becomes sub-paragraph (1).

(3) After that sub-paragraph insert—

"(2) If it appears to Her Majesty that in the circumstances it is desirable to do so, Her Majesty may, before the end of the term for which a person is appointed as non-executive director, extend the person's term of office on one occasion for a specified period of not more than 6 months.

(3) If a person whose term of office is extended under sub-paragraph (2) is subsequently re-appointed as non-executive director—

(a) the length of the term of his or her re-appointment (or, if the person is re-appointed more than once, of the first re-appointment following the extension) is to be reduced by a period equal to the extension, but

(b) the term of that re-appointment may itself be extended under sub-paragraph (2)."

3 Abolition of Oversight Committee

(1) The Bank of England Act 1998 is amended as follows.

(2) In section 2(2) (functions of court of directors)—

(a) the words from "determining the Bank's objectives" to the end become paragraph (a);

(b) after that paragraph insert—

"(b) the functions mentioned in section 3A(2) (the "oversight functions")."

(3) In section 3A (Oversight Committee)—

(a) omit subsection (1);

(b) in subsection (2), in the words before paragraph (a) for "functions of the Oversight Committee" substitute "oversight functions of the court of directors";

(c) in subsection (2)(d) for "Oversight Committee" substitute "court of directors";

(d) omit subsection (3);

(e) in the heading for "Committee" substitute "functions of court of directors".

(4) Omit section 3B (Oversight Committee: procedure).

(5) In section 3C (reviews) after subsection (1) insert—

"(1A) Where they consider that to do so would contribute to the discharge by the court of directors of any of its oversight functions, the non-executive directors of the Bank (or a majority of them) may arrange—
(a) for a review to be conducted under this section in relation to any matter by a person appointed by those directors, and
(b) for the person conducting the review to make one or more reports to the court of directors."

4 Functions of non-executive directors

(1) Schedule 1 to the Bank of England Act 1998 (court of directors) is amended as follows.

(2) In paragraph 14 (remuneration)—
(a) at the beginning insert—

"(A1) The remuneration of the Governor and Deputy Governors of the Bank is to be determined by a sub-committee of the court of directors consisting of 3 or more non-executive directors of the Bank.";

(b) in sub-paragraph (1) for "the Oversight Committee" substitute "that sub-committee".

5 Financial stability strategy

(1) Paragraph 11 of Schedule 1 to the Bank of England Act 1998 (matters which may be delegated by court of directors) is amended as follows.

(2) In sub-paragraph (2) after "paragraph" insert—
"(a) include duties and powers conferred on the court of directors by section 9A (financial stability strategy), but
(b) except as mentioned in paragraph (a),".

(3) After sub-paragraph (2) insert—

"(3) The court of directors retains responsibility for a duty or power which it delegates under this paragraph."

6 Financial Policy Committee: status and membership

(1) Section 9B(1) of the Bank of England Act 1998 (Financial Policy Committee) is amended as follows.

(2) In the words before paragraph (a), for "sub-committee of the court of directors" substitute "committee".

(3) For paragraph (b) substitute—
"(b) the Deputy Governor for financial stability,
(ba) the Deputy Governor for markets and banking,
(bb) the Deputy Governor for monetary policy,
(bc) the Deputy Governor for prudential regulation,".

(4) In paragraph (e) for "4" substitute "5".

7 Monetary Policy Committee: membership

(1) Section 13 of the Bank of England Act 1998 (Monetary Policy Committee) is amended as follows.

(2) In subsection (2)—

(a) after paragraph (aa) insert—

"(aaa) the Deputy Governor for markets and banking,";

(b) in paragraph (b) for "2 members" substitute "one member (to be known as the Chief Economist of the Bank)".

(3) For subsection (3) substitute—

"(3) The member appointed under subsection (2)(b) shall be a person who carries out monetary policy analysis within the Bank."

(4) For subsection (4) substitute—

"(4) Before appointing a person under subsection (2)(c) the Chancellor of the Exchequer must—

(a) be satisfied that the person has knowledge or experience which is likely to be relevant to the Committee's functions, and

(b) consider whether the person has any financial or other interests that could substantially affect the functions as member that it would be proper for the person to discharge."

8 Monetary Policy Committee: procedure

(1) The Bank of England Act 1998 is amended as follows.

(2) In section 15(1) (publication of Monetary Policy Committee minutes: usual rule)—

(a) for "After" substitute "As soon as reasonably practicable after";

(b) omit the words from "before" to the end.

(3) In section 15(3) (publication of Monetary Policy Committee minutes: special cases)—

(a) for "before the end of the period of 6 weeks beginning with the day of" substitute "as soon as reasonably practicable after";

(b) for "before the end of the period of 6 weeks beginning with the day on which" substitute "as soon as reasonably practicable after".

(4) In paragraph 10 of Schedule 3 (meetings of Monetary Policy Committee)—

(a) in sub-paragraph (1) for "once a month" substitute "8 times in each calendar year";

(b) after sub-paragraph (1) insert—

"(1A) The Committee shall meet at least once in any 10 week period."

(5) In paragraph 11 of Schedule 3 (proceedings of Monetary Policy Committee: quorum) —

(a) in sub-paragraph (2) for "whom" to the end substitute "whom—

(a) one must be the Governor of the Bank or the Deputy Governor for monetary policy,

(b) unless both those mentioned in paragraph (a) are present, one must be either the Deputy Governor for financial stability or the Deputy Governor for markets and banking.";

(b) in sub-paragraph (6) after "(5)" insert "and paragraph 13B".

(6) In Schedule 3, after paragraph 13A insert—

"13B (1) If a member of the Committee ("M") has any direct or indirect interest (including any reasonably likely future interest) in any dealing or business which falls to be considered by the Committee—

(a) M must disclose that interest to the Committee when it considers the dealing or business, and

(b) the Committee must decide whether M is to be permitted to participate in any proceedings of the Committee relating to any question arising from its consideration of the dealing or business, and if so to what extent and subject to what conditions (if any).

(2) The Bank must issue and maintain a code of practice describing how members of the Committee and the Committee are to comply with sub-paragraph (1).

(3) The Bank may at any time revise or replace the code.

(4) Before issuing, revising or replacing the code, the Bank must consult the Treasury.

(5) The Bank must publish the current version of the code in whatever manner it sees fit.

(6) The Committee must comply with the code when taking decisions under sub-paragraph (1)(b)."

Financial arrangements

9 Audit

In the Bank of England Act 1998, after section 7 insert—

"7ZA Audit: role of Comptroller and Auditor General

(1) Before appointing an auditor or auditors under section 7(5), the Bank must consult the Comptroller and Auditor General ("the Comptroller").

(2) The auditor or auditors appointed by the Bank must consult the Comptroller on the scope, timing and direction of the audit and on any audit plan (or any material revisions to an audit plan).

(3) The Comptroller—

(a) has a right of access at any reasonable time to any document relating to the audit of the Bank's accounts which the Comptroller may reasonably require, and

(b) may require any person holding or accountable for any such document to provide such information and explanation as are reasonably necessary.

(4) Subsection (3) applies only to documents in the custody or under the control of the Bank.

(5) An obligation imposed on a person as a result of the exercise of the powers conferred by subsection (3) is enforceable by injunction or, in Scotland, by an order for specific performance under section 45 of the Court of Session Act 1988.

(6) The Comptroller (or a person nominated by the Comptroller) may attend any proceedings of the Bank's audit committee which are concerned with the audit of the Bank's accounts.

(7) The "Bank's audit committee" means the committee or sub-committee within the Bank for the time being having responsibilities relating to the audit of the Bank's accounts."

10 Activities indemnified by Treasury

In the Bank of England Act 1998, after section 7A insert—

"7B Reports on Bank activities indemnified by Treasury

(1) This section applies where the Treasury give an indemnity or guarantee to the Bank in respect of an activity or series of activities undertaken by the Bank.

(2) The Treasury may direct the Bank to prepare a financial report in relation to the activity or series of activities to which the indemnity or guarantee relates.

(3) A direction under subsection (2) may include directions as to—
- (a) the financial years for which a report is to be prepared,
- (b) the information to be contained in the report and the manner in which it is to be presented, and
- (c) the methods and principles according to which any statement of financial information to be contained in the report is to be prepared.

(4) A direction under subsection (2) may be revoked by a further direction.

(5) The Bank must send any report that it prepares under subsection (2) to the Treasury.

(6) The Treasury may send the report to the Comptroller and Auditor General ("the Comptroller") for review.

(7) The review is to consider such matters as may be agreed between the Comptroller and the Treasury.

(8) The Comptroller—
- (a) has a right of access at any reasonable time to any document the Comptroller may reasonably require for the purposes of the review, and
- (b) may require any person holding or accountable for any such document to provide such information and explanation as are reasonably necessary.

(9) Subsection (8) applies only to documents in the custody or under the control of—

(a) the Bank;

(b) the auditor or auditors appointed by the Bank under section 7(5).

(10) An obligation imposed on a person as a result of the exercise of the powers conferred by subsection (8) is enforceable by injunction or, in Scotland, by an order for specific performance under section 45 of the Court of Session Act 1988.

7C Accounts of Bank companies carrying on activities indemnified by Treasury

(1) This section applies where the Treasury give an indemnity or guarantee to a company ("the company") in which the Bank has an interest, in respect of an activity or series of activities undertaken by the company.

(2) The Treasury may direct the company to send to the Comptroller and Auditor General ("the Comptroller") accounts prepared by it in accordance with the Companies Act 2006 and any direction given by the Bank under section 7A(1).

(3) A direction given under subsection (2)—

(a) may relate to all financial years, or to financial years specified in the direction;

(b) may be revoked by a further direction.

(4) Where a direction given under subsection (2) has effect in relation to a financial year, the company is exempt from the requirements of Part 16 of the Companies Act 2006 (audit) for that financial year, and its balance sheet must include a statement to that effect.

(5) The Comptroller must examine any accounts sent to the Comptroller under this section with a view to satisfying himself or herself that the accounts have been properly prepared in all material respects in accordance with the bases of preparation identified in the accounts.

(6) After completing the examination the Comptroller must—

(a) certify the accounts and issue a report,

(b) send the certified accounts and the report to the Treasury, and

(c) if not satisfied that the accounts have been properly prepared in all material respects in accordance with the bases of preparation identified in the accounts, report to the House of Commons.

(7) The Treasury must lay the copy of the certified accounts and the report before Parliament.

(8) For the purposes of this section, the Bank has an interest in a company if—

(a) the Bank, or a nominee of the Bank, is a member of the company, or

(b) the company is a subsidiary undertaking of the Bank, within the meaning of section 1162 of the Companies Act 2006."

11 Examinations and reviews

In the Bank of England Act 1998, after section 7C (inserted by section 10) insert—

"7D Examination by Comptroller and Auditor General

(1) The Comptroller and Auditor General ("the Comptroller") may carry out examinations into—
(a) the economy, efficiency and effectiveness with which the Bank has used its resources in discharging its functions;
(b) the economy, efficiency and effectiveness with which a Bank company has used its resources in discharging its functions.

(2) An examination under this section may be limited to such functions (however described) of the Bank or the Bank company as the Comptroller considers appropriate.

(3) An examination under this section is not to be concerned with the merits of the Bank's policy objectives.

(4) An examination under this section is not to be concerned with the merits of—
(a) policy decisions taken by the Financial Policy Committee, the Monetary Policy Committee or the Prudential Regulation Committee;
(b) policy decisions taken by a committee or other body within the Bank for the time being having responsibilities for the supervision of payment systems, settlement systems or clearing houses, so far as the decisions relate to that supervision.

(5) Subject to subsection (6), an examination under this section is not to be concerned with the merits of policy decisions taken by a committee or other body within the Bank for the time being having responsibilities for the exercise of any of the Bank's resolution functions, so far as the decisions relate to those functions.

(6) Where the Bank has exercised relevant resolution functions in relation to a financial institution, subsection (5) does not prevent an examination under this section being concerned with the merits of policy decisions within that subsection which are relevant to the Bank's exercise of its resolution functions in relation to that institution (whether or not those policy decisions are also relevant to other financial institutions).

(7) "Relevant resolution functions" are—
(a) any of the stabilisation powers;
(b) any of the Bank's functions (other than its functions as the Prudential Regulation Authority) under or by virtue of—
(i) Part 2 or 3, or section 233, of the Banking Act 2009,
(ii) Part 6 of the Financial Services (Banking Reform) Act 2013.

(8) Before carrying out an examination under this section, the Comptroller must consult the court of directors of the Bank.

(9) The Comptroller may report to the House of Commons the results of any examination carried out by the Comptroller under this section.

(10) For the purposes of this section—
"Bank company" means—

(a) a company which is a subsidiary undertaking of the Bank, within the meaning of section 1162 of the Companies Act 2006;

(b) a company not within paragraph (a) in respect of which a direction under section 7C(2) has effect;

"resolution functions" means the Bank's functions (other than its functions as the Prudential Regulation Authority) under or by virtue of—

(a) Parts 1 to 3, and section 233, of the Banking Act 2009,

(b) Part 6 of the Financial Services (Banking Reform) Act 2013,

(c) the Bank Recovery and Resolution (No. 2) Order 2014 (S.I. 2014/3348);

"stabilisation powers" has the same meaning as in the Banking Act 2009 (see section 1(4) of that Act).

(11) Section 6 of the National Audit Act 1983 (Comptroller may carry out economy, efficiency and effectiveness examinations) does not apply to the Bank or a Bank company.

7E Memorandum of understanding

(1) The Bank and the Comptroller must prepare and maintain a memorandum of understanding about examinations under section 7D.

(2) The memorandum must in particular include provision—

(a) as to functions of the Bank in respect of which the Comptroller will not usually consider it appropriate to carry out an examination;

(b) identifying the committees or other bodies referred to in section 7D(4)(b) and (5);

(c) establishing a procedure for resolving in a timely fashion any dispute between the Bank and the Comptroller as to whether a matter is (under section 7D(3) to (6)) a matter with which an examination under section 7D is not to be concerned;

(d) for the publication of the views of the Bank and the Comptroller as to whether a matter is such a matter, in cases where a dispute between them cannot be resolved.

7F Review by the Treasury

(1) The Treasury may appoint an independent person to conduct a review of the economy, efficiency and effectiveness with which the Bank has used its resources in discharging its functions as the Prudential Regulation Authority.

(2) "Independent" means appearing to the Treasury to be independent of the Bank.

(3) A review under this section may be limited to such of the Bank's functions as the Prudential Regulation Authority (however described) as the Treasury may specify in appointing the person to conduct it.

(4) A review under this section is not to be concerned with the merits of the Bank's general policy or principles in pursuing the Bank's objectives (including its objectives as the Prudential Regulation Authority).

(5) On completion of the review, the person conducting it must make a written report to the Treasury—

(a) setting out the result of the review, and

(b) making such recommendations (if any) as the person considers appropriate.

(6) A copy of the report must be—

(a) laid before Parliament, and

(b) published in such manner as the Treasury think fit.

(7) Any expenses reasonably incurred in the conduct of the review are to be met by the Treasury out of money provided by Parliament.

7G Right to obtain documents and information

(1) A person conducting an examination under section 7D or a review under section 7F—

(a) has a right of access at any reasonable time to any document the person may reasonably require for the purposes of the examination or review, and

(b) may require any person holding or accountable for any such document to provide such information and explanation as are reasonably necessary for that purpose.

(2) Subsection (1) applies to documents in the custody or under the control of—

(a) the Bank;

(b) the auditor or auditors appointed by the Bank under section 7(5).

(3) In the case of an examination under section 7D(1)(b), subsection (1) also applies to documents in the custody or under the control of—

(a) the company to which the examination relates;

(b) the auditor or auditors of that company.

(4) An obligation imposed on a person as a result of the exercise of the powers conferred by subsection (1) is enforceable by injunction or, in Scotland, by an order for specific performance under section 45 of the Court of Session Act 1988.

7H Restriction on disclosing information

Section 353A of the Financial Services and Markets Act 2000 (FCA not to disclose certain information received from the Bank) applies in relation to the Comptroller and Auditor General and the National Audit Office as it applies in relation to the Financial Conduct Authority."

Prudential regulation

12 Bank to act as Prudential Regulation Authority

In the Financial Services and Markets Act 2000, for section 2A substitute—

"2A The Prudential Regulation Authority

(1) The "Prudential Regulation Authority" is the Bank of England.

(2) The Bank's functions as the Prudential Regulation Authority—
  (a) are to be exercised by the Bank acting through its Prudential Regulation Committee (see Part 3A of the Bank of England Act 1998), and
  (b) are not exercisable by the Bank in any other way.

(3) References in this Act or any other enactment to the Prudential Regulation Authority do not include the Bank of England acting otherwise than in its capacity as the Prudential Regulation Authority.

(4) References in this Act to the Bank of England do not (unless otherwise provided) include the Bank acting in its capacity as the Prudential Regulation Authority.

(5) Subsections (3) and (4) do not apply to this section.

(6) Subsection (4) does not apply for the interpretation of references to the court of directors of the Bank of England, or to a Deputy Governor or committee of the Bank.

(7) The Prudential Regulation Authority is referred to in this Act as the PRA.

2AB Functions of the PRA

(1) The PRA is to have the functions conferred on it by or under this Act.

(2) Schedule 1ZB makes provision about functions of the PRA.

(3) References in this Act or any other enactment to functions conferred on the PRA by or under this Act include references to functions conferred on the PRA by or under—
  (a) the Insolvency Act 1986,
  (b) the Banking Act 2009,
  (c) the Financial Services Act 2012, or
  (d) a qualifying EU provision that is specified, or of a description specified, for the purposes of this subsection by the Treasury by order."

13 Prudential Regulation Committee

(1) The Bank of England Act 1998 is amended as follows.

(2) After Part 3 insert—

"PART 3A

PRUDENTIAL REGULATION

30A Prudential Regulation Committee

(1) There is to be a committee of the Bank known as the Prudential Regulation Committee of the Bank of England.

(2) The Prudential Regulation Committee is to consist of—
- (a) the Governor of the Bank,
- (b) the Deputy Governor for financial stability,
- (c) the Deputy Governor for markets and banking,
- (d) the Deputy Governor for prudential regulation,
- (e) the Chief Executive of the Financial Conduct Authority,
- (f) one member appointed by the Governor of the Bank with the approval of the Chancellor of the Exchequer, and
- (g) at least 6 members appointed by the Chancellor of the Exchequer.

(3) The functions of the Prudential Regulation Committee are—
- (a) its functions by virtue of section 2A of the Financial Services and Markets Act 2000 (which provides for the Bank's functions as the Prudential Regulation Authority to be exercised by the Bank acting through the Prudential Regulation Committee), and
- (b) the functions conferred on it by this Act.

(4) Schedule 6A has effect with respect to the Prudential Regulation Committee.

30B Recommendations by Treasury

(1) The Treasury may at any time by notice in writing to the Prudential Regulation Committee make recommendations to the Committee about aspects of the economic policy of Her Majesty's Government to which the Committee should have regard—
- (a) when considering how to advance the objectives of the Prudential Regulation Authority, and
- (b) when considering the application of the regulatory principles set out in section 3B of the Financial Services and Markets Act 2000.

(2) The Treasury must make recommendations under subsection (1) at least once in each Parliament.

(3) The Treasury must—
- (a) publish in such manner as they think fit any notice given under subsection (1), and
- (b) lay a copy of it before Parliament.

30C Operational independence

(1) The Bank must make arrangements to ensure compliance with—

(a) article 4.7 of the capital requirements directive, and
(b) article 3.3 of the recovery and resolution directive,

(which require resolution functions and supervisory functions to be operationally independent of one another).

(2) The Bank must prepare and issue a statement of its arrangements under subsection (1).

(3) If there are material changes to the arrangements, it must prepare and issue a revised statement.

(4) The Bank must consult the Treasury before issuing a statement under subsection (2) or a revised statement under subsection (3).

(5) If it appears to the Treasury that any action proposed to be taken by the Bank would be incompatible with obligations of the United Kingdom under the provisions mentioned in subsection (1)(a) or (b), the Treasury may direct the Bank not to take that action.

(6) If it appears to the Treasury that any action which the Bank has power to take is required for the purpose of implementing those obligations, the Treasury may direct the Bank to take that action.

(7) In this section—

"the capital requirements directive" means Directive 2013/36/EU of the European Parliament and of the Council of 26 June 2013 on access to the activity of credit institutions and the prudential supervision of credit institutions and investment firms;

"the recovery and resolution directive" means Directive 2014/59/EU of the European Parliament and of the Council of 15 May 2014 establishing a framework for the recovery and resolution of credit institutions and investment firms."

(3) Before Schedule 7 insert the Schedule 6A set out in Schedule 1 to this Act.

14 Accounts relating to Bank's functions as Prudential Regulation Authority

(1) Section 7 of the Bank of England Act 1998 (accounts) is amended as follows.

(2) After subsection (2) insert—

"(2A) The Bank shall also prepare for each of its financial years a statement of accounts in relation to—

(a) income received and assets accrued by the Bank by virtue of its functions as the Prudential Regulation Authority, and
(b) expenses and liabilities incurred by the Bank by virtue of its functions as the Prudential Regulation Authority."

(3) After subsection (4) insert—

"(4A) In preparing a statement under subsection (2A) the Bank must comply with any directions given by the Treasury as to—

(a) the information to be contained in the statement and the manner in which it is to be presented, and

(b) the methods and principles according to which the statement is to be prepared."

(4) In subsection (5), after "subsection (2)" insert "or (2A)".

(5) After subsection (5) insert—

"(5A) The auditor's report on a statement under subsection (2A) must state whether the auditor is satisfied that the Bank has complied with the requirements of Part 3 of Schedule 1ZB to the Financial Services and Markets Act 2000 (Prudential Regulation Authority fees and penalties)."

(6) In subsection (6), after "subsection (2)" insert "or (2A)".

(7) After subsection (8) insert—

"(8A) A direction under subsection (4A) or a notice under subsection (7) may be revoked by a further direction or notice."

15 Transfer of property etc to Bank

(1) The property, rights and liabilities to which the company is entitled or subject immediately before this section comes into force transfer to and vest in the Bank of England, in its capacity as the Prudential Regulation Authority.

(2) Subsection (1) has effect in spite of any provision (of whatever nature) that would otherwise prevent, penalise or restrict the transfer of the property, rights or liabilities.

(3) In particular, it has effect regardless of a contravention, liability or interference with an interest or right that would otherwise exist by reason of such a provision having effect in relation to the terms on which the company is entitled to the property or right, or subject to the liability, in question.

(4) A certificate by the Chancellor of the Exchequer that anything specified in the certificate has vested in the Bank of England under this section is conclusive evidence for all purposes of that fact.

(5) In this section "the company" means the body corporate originally incorporated as the Prudential Regulation Authority Limited and renamed as the Prudential Regulation Authority by section 2A of the Financial Services and Markets Act 2000 (as it had effect before section 12 came into force).

Consequential and transitional provision

16 Amendments relating to Part 1

Schedule 2 makes amendments relating to this Part.

17 Saving and transitional provision relating to Part 1

Schedule 3 makes saving and transitional provision relating to this Part.

PART 2

FINANCIAL SERVICES

The regulators

18 Appointment of Financial Conduct Authority chief executive

In Schedule 1ZA to the Financial Services and Markets Act 2000 (the Financial Conduct Authority), after paragraph 2 insert—

"2A (1) The term of office of a person appointed as chief executive under paragraph 2(2)(b) must not begin before—

(a) the person has, in connection with the appointment, appeared before the Treasury Committee of the House of Commons, or

(b) (if earlier) the end of the period of 3 months beginning with the day on which the appointment is made.

(2) Sub-paragraph (1) does not apply if the person is appointed as chief executive on an acting basis, pending a further appointment being made.

(3) The reference to the Treasury Committee of the House of Commons—

(a) if the name of that Committee is changed, is a reference to that Committee by its new name, and

(b) if the functions of that Committee (or substantially corresponding functions) become functions of a different Committee of the House of Commons, is to be treated as a reference to the Committee by which the functions are exercisable.

(4) Any question arising under sub-paragraph (3) is to be determined by the Speaker of the House of Commons."

19 Treasury recommendations to Financial Conduct Authority

In Chapter 1 of Part 1A of the Financial Services and Markets Act 2000 (the Financial Conduct Authority), after section 1J insert—

"Recommendations

1JA Recommendations by Treasury in connection with general duties

(1) The Treasury may at any time by notice in writing to the FCA make recommendations to the FCA about aspects of the economic policy of Her Majesty's Government to which the FCA should have regard when considering—

(a) how to act in a way which is compatible with its strategic objective,

(b) how to advance one or more of its operational objectives,

(c) how to discharge the duty in section 1B(4) (duty to promote effective competition in the interests of consumers),

(d) the application of the regulatory principles in section 3B, and

(e) the matter mentioned in section 1B(5)(b) (importance of taking action to minimise the extent to which it is possible for a business to be used for a purpose connected with financial crime).

(2) The Treasury must make recommendations under subsection (1) at least once in each Parliament.

(3) The Treasury must—

(a) publish in such manner as they think fit any notice given under subsection (1), and

(b) lay a copy of it before Parliament."

20 Regulatory principles: diversity

(1) Section 3B of the Financial Services and Markets Act 2000 (regulatory principles to be applied by both regulators) is amended as follows.

(2) In subsection (1)(f) after "persons" insert "(including different kinds of person such as mutual societies and other kinds of business organisation)".

(3) After subsection (3) insert—

"(3A) Mutual society" has the same meaning as in section 138K."

Conduct of persons working in financial services sector

21 Extension of relevant authorised persons regime to all authorised persons

Schedule 4 makes provision extending to authorised persons provisions of Part 5 of the Financial Services and Markets Act 2000 (performance of regulated activities) which now apply only to relevant authorised persons.

22 Rules about controlled functions: power to make transitional provision

(1) The Financial Services and Markets Act 2000 is amended as follows.

(2) After section 59A insert—

"59AB Specifying functions as controlled functions: transitional provision

(1) In relation to rules made by the FCA or the PRA under section 59, the power conferred by section 137T(c) to make transitional provision includes in particular power—

(a) to provide for anything done under this Part in relation to controlled functions of a particular description to be treated as having been done in relation to controlled functions of a different description;

(b) to provide for anything done under this Part (including any application or order made, any requirement imposed and any approval or notice given) to cease to have effect, to continue to have effect, or to continue to have effect with modifications, or subject to time limits or conditions;

(c) to provide for rules made by the regulator making the rules under section 59 to apply with modifications;

(d) to make saving provision.

(2) The Treasury may by regulations make whatever incidental, consequential, transitional, supplemental or saving provision the Treasury consider appropriate in connection with the making of rules by the FCA or the PRA under section 59.

(3) Regulations under subsection (2) may—

(a) confer functions on the FCA or the PRA (including the function of making rules);

(b) modify, exclude or apply (with or without modifications) any primary or subordinate legislation (including any provision of, or made under, this Act)."

(3) In section 429(2B) (regulations subject to affirmative procedure) for "contain" substitute "contain—

(a) provision made under section 59AB(2) which modifies, excludes or applies with modifications any provision of primary legislation;".

23 Administration of senior managers regime

(1) The Financial Services and Markets Act 2000 is amended as follows.

(2) In section 62A(4) (changes in responsibilities of senior managers), at the end of the definition of "the appropriate regulator" insert ", except that the reference in section 60(9)(b) to subsection (3) is to be treated as a reference to subsection (2) of this section".

(3) In section 63ZA (variation of senior manager's approval at request of authorised person)—

(a) in subsection (1), for "application for approval under section 59 is granted" substitute "approval under section 59 has effect";

(b) after subsection (1) insert—

"(1A) Where an approval under section 59 has effect for a limited period, the authorised person concerned may apply to the appropriate regulator to vary the approval by—

(a) varying the period for which the approval is to have effect, or

(b) removing the limit on the period for which the approval is to have effect.";

(c) in subsection (2)(a) the words from "whichever" to the end become sub-paragraph (i), and at the end of that sub-paragraph insert ", or

(ii) if the condition has been varied before (under this section or section 63ZB), whichever of the FCA or the PRA last varied it;";

(d) after subsection (2)(b) insert—

"(c) in the case of an application for variation of an approval in a way described in subsection (1A), means—

(i) whichever of the FCA or the PRA imposed the limit on the period for which the approval has effect, or

(ii) if the limit has been varied before (under this section or section 63ZB), whichever of the FCA or the PRA last varied it.";

(e) in subsection (3) for "which was imposed" substitute ", or a limit on the period for which an approval has effect, which was imposed (or last varied)";

(f) after subsection (7) insert—

"(7A) An application may not be made under this section for the variation or removal of a condition, or a limit on the period for which an approval has effect, where the condition or limit has effect by virtue of section 66.";

(g) in subsection (8), after "section 62" insert ", but as if in subsections (2), (3) and (4) the words ", or to grant the application subject to conditions or for a limited period (or both)" were omitted".

(4) In section 63ZB (variation of senior manager's approval on initiative of regulator)—

(a) omit the "or" at the end of subsection (3)(c);

(b) at the beginning of subsection (3)(d) insert "where the approval has effect for an unlimited period,";

(c) at the end of subsection (3)(d) insert ", or

(e) where the approval has effect for a limited period, varying that period or removing the limit on the period for which the approval is to have effect.";

(d) after subsection (4) insert—

"(4A) Before one regulator varies an approval which was last varied by the other regulator, it must consult the other regulator."

(5) In section 204A (meaning of appropriate regulator)—

(a) in subsection (3)(d) for the words from "the authorised person" to the end substitute "the revised statement of responsibilities is to be provided to the PRA only;";

(b) in subsection (3A), after paragraph (b) insert—

"(ba) a requirement under section 62A(2) where the revised statement of responsibilities is to be provided to the FCA and the PRA;".

24 Rules of conduct

(1) The Financial Services and Markets Act 2000 is amended as follows.

(2) In section 64A (power of FCA and PRA to make rules of conduct)—

(a) in subsection (1) after paragraph (b) insert—

"(c) persons who are directors of authorised persons.";

(b) in subsection (2) after paragraph (c) insert—

"(d) persons who are directors of PRA-authorised persons.";

(c) omit the "and" at the end of subsection (5)(a);

(d) after subsection (5)(a) insert—

"(ab) in the case of a person who is a director of an authorised person but is not an approved person, that authorised person, and";

(e) after subsection (6) insert—

"(7) In this section "director", in relation to an authorised person, means a member of the board of directors, or if there is no such board, the equivalent body responsible for the management of the authorised person concerned."

(3) In section 64B (responsibilities of authorised persons in relation to rules of conduct)—

(a) omit the "and" at the end of subsection (4)(a);

(b) at the end of subsection (4)(b) insert ", and

(c) any person who is a director of the authorised person.";

(c) omit subsection (5);

(d) after subsection (6) insert—

"(6A) In this section "director", in relation to an authorised person, has the same meaning as in section 64A."

25 Misconduct

(1) The Financial Services and Markets Act 2000 is amended as follows.

(2) In section 66A (misconduct: action by FCA)—

(a) omit the "or" at the end of subsection (2)(b)(i);

(b) at the end of subsection (2)(b)(ii) insert ", or

(iii) a director of an authorised person.";

(c) omit the "or" at the end of subsection (3)(b)(i);

(d) at the end of subsection (3)(b)(ii) insert ", or

(iii) a director of the authorised person.";

(e) omit the "and" at the end of subsection (5)(b);

(f) at the end of subsection (5)(c) insert ", and

(d) the senior manager did not take such steps as a person in the senior manager's position could reasonably be expected to take to avoid the contravention occurring (or continuing).";

(g) omit subsection (6);

(h) in subsection (8) after the definition of "approved person" insert—

"""director", in relation to an authorised person, has the same meaning as in section 64A;".

(3) In section 66B (misconduct: action by PRA)—

(a) omit the "or" at the end of subsection (2)(b)(i);

(b) at the end of subsection (2)(b)(ii) insert ", or

(iii) a director of a PRA-authorised person.";

(c) omit the "or" at the end of subsection (3)(b)(i);

(d) at the end of subsection (3)(b)(ii) insert ", or

(iii) a director of the PRA-authorised person.";

(e) omit the "and" at the end of subsection (5)(b);

(f) at the end of subsection (5)(c) insert ", and

(d) the senior manager did not take such steps as a person in the senior manager's position could reasonably be expected to take to avoid the contravention occurring (or continuing).";

(g) omit subsection (6);

(h) in subsection (8) after the definition of "approved person" insert—

""director", in relation to an authorised person, has the same meaning as in section 64A;".

26 Decisions causing a financial institution to fail: meaning of insolvency

(1) Section 37 of the Financial Services (Banking Reform) Act 2013 (interpretation of section 36) is amended as follows.

(2) In subsection (10)—

(a) after paragraph (c) insert—

"(ca) building society insolvency,

(cb) investment bank insolvency,";

(b) after paragraph (e) insert—

"(ea) building society special administration,".

(3) After subsection (10) insert—

"(11) For the purposes of subsection (10)—

"bank administration" has the same meaning as in the Banking Act 2009 (see section 136 of that Act);

"bank insolvency" has the same meaning as in that Act (see section 90 of that Act);

"building society insolvency" and "building society special administration" have the same meaning as in the Building Societies Act 1986 (see section 119 of that Act);

"investment bank insolvency" means any procedure established by regulations under section 233 of the Banking Act 2009."

Enforceability of agreements

27 Enforceability of agreements relating to credit

(1) Section 26A of the Financial Services and Markets Act 2000 (agreements relating to credit) is amended as follows.

(2) In subsection (4)—

(a) the words from "has" to the end become paragraph (a);

(b) after that paragraph insert—

"(b) is an appointed representative in relation to that activity,

(c) is an exempt person in relation to that activity, or

(d) is a person to whom, as a result of Part 20, the general prohibition does not apply in relation to that activity."

(3) In subsection (5)—

(a) the words from "the agreement" (in the third place they occur) to the end become paragraph (a) (and the existing paragraphs (a) and (b) become sub-paragraphs (i) and (ii) of that paragraph);

(b) after that paragraph insert—

"(b) that person is an appointed representative in relation to that activity,

(c) that person is an exempt person in relation to that activity, or

(d) that person is a person to whom, as a result of Part 20, the general prohibition does not apply in relation to that activity."

28 Enforceability of agreements made through unauthorised persons

(1) Section 27 of the Financial Services and Markets Act 2000 (agreements made through unauthorised persons) is amended as follows.

(2) After subsection (1) insert—

"(1ZA) But this section does not apply to a regulated credit agreement or a regulated consumer hire agreement unless the provider knows before the agreement is made that the third party had some involvement in the making of the agreement or matters preparatory to its making."

(3) In subsection (1A) for "The agreement" substitute "An agreement to which this section applies".

(4) After subsection (4) insert—

"(5) For the purposes of subsection (1ZA)—

"regulated consumer hire agreement" has the meaning given by article 60N of the Financial Services and Markets Act 2000 (Regulated Activities) Order 2001 (S.I. 2001/544);

"regulated credit agreement" has the meaning given by article 60B of that Order."

Illegal money lending

29 Illegal money lending

(1) The Financial Services and Markets Act 2000 is amended as follows.

(2) After Part 20A insert—

"PART 20B

ILLEGAL MONEY LENDING

333S Financial assistance for action against illegal money lending

(1) The Treasury may make grants or loans, or give any other form of financial assistance, to any person for the purpose of taking action against illegal money lending.

(2) Taking action against illegal money lending includes—

(a) investigating illegal money lending and offences connected with illegal money lending;

(b) prosecuting, or taking other enforcement action in respect of, illegal money lending and offences connected with illegal money lending;

(c) providing education, information and advice about illegal money lending, and providing support to victims of illegal money lending;

(d) undertaking or commissioning research into the effectiveness of activities of the kind described in paragraphs (a) to (c);

(e) providing advice, assistance and support (including financial support) to, and oversight of, persons engaged in activities of the kind described in paragraphs (a) to (c).

(3) A grant, loan or other form of financial assistance under subsection (1) may be made or given on such terms as the Treasury consider appropriate.

(4) "Illegal money lending" means carrying on a regulated activity within article 60B of the Financial Services and Markets Act 2000 (Regulated Activities) Order 2001 (S.I. 2001/544) (regulated credit agreements) in circumstances which constitute an authorisation offence.

333T Funding of action against illegal money lending

(1) The Treasury must, from time to time, notify the FCA of the amount of the Treasury's illegal money lending costs.

(2) The FCA must make rules requiring authorised persons, or any specified class of authorised person, to pay to the FCA specified amounts, or amounts calculated in a specified way, with a view to recovering the amount notified under subsection (1).

(3) The amounts to be paid under the rules may include a component to recover the expenses of the FCA in collecting the payments ("collection costs").

(4) Before the FCA publishes a draft of the rules it must consult the Treasury.

(5) The rules may be made only with the consent of the Treasury.

(6) The Treasury may notify the FCA of matters that they will take into account when deciding whether or not to give consent for the purposes of subsection (5).

(7) The FCA must have regard to any matters notified under subsection (6) before publishing a draft of rules to be made under this section.

(8) The FCA must pay to the Treasury the amounts that it receives under rules made under this section apart from amounts in respect of its collection costs (which it may keep).

(9) The Treasury must pay into the Consolidated Fund the amounts received by them under subsection (8).

(10) In this section the "Treasury's illegal money lending costs" means the expenses incurred, or expected to be incurred, by the Treasury—

(a) in connection with providing grants, loans, or other financial assistance to any person (under section 333S or otherwise) for the purpose of taking action against illegal money lending;

(b) in undertaking or commissioning research relating to taking action against illegal money lending.

(11) The Treasury may by regulations amend the definition of the "Treasury's illegal money lending costs".

(12) In this section "illegal money lending" and "taking action against illegal money lending" have the same meaning as in section 333S."

(3) In section 138F (notification of rules), for "or 333R" substitute ", 333R or 333T".

(4) In section 138I (consultation by FCA)—

(a) in subsection (6), after paragraph (cb) insert—

"(cc) section 333T;";

(b) in subsection (10)(a), for "or 333R" substitute ", 333R or 333T".

(5) In section 429(2) (regulations subject to affirmative procedure), for "or 333R" substitute ", 333R or 333T".

(6) In paragraph 23 of Schedule 1ZA (FCA fees rules)—

(a) in sub-paragraph (1) for "and 333R" substitute ", 333R and 333T";

(b) in sub-paragraph (2ZA)(b) for "section 333R" substitute "sections 333R and 333T".

Money laundering

30 Money laundering

(1) In any regulations or orders transposing money laundering measures contained within Directive (EU) 2015/849 of the European Parliament and of the Council of 20 May 2015 (or in relation to any subsequent EU amending or successor measure) the Secretary of State shall have a duty to ensure, insofar as such regulations or orders relate to institutions regulated by the Financial Conduct Authority—

(a) reasonable regard and due prominence is given to—

(i) recital 33,

(ii) Article 13(2),

(iii) Article 15, and

(iv) Article 16 and Annex II;

(b) clarity is achieved with respect to the meaning and interpretation of "prominent public function" in the context of money laundering;

(c) reasonable regard and due prominence is given to Article 22 which recognises that a politically exposed person may have no prominent public function; and

(d) any interpretation of "adequate" in Article 20(b)(ii), and "enhanced" in Article 20(b)(iii) takes account of, and gives due prominence to, the provisions in Article 13 on risk sensitivity.

(2) The Financial Services and Markets Act 2000 is amended as follows.

(3) After Part 20B insert—

"PART 20C

MONEY LAUNDERING

333U Money laundering: guidance

(1) The FCA must, prior to relevant regulations coming into force, issue guidance to regulated entities on the definition of one or more categories of politically exposed persons ("PEPs").

(2) Guidance under subsection (1) must include, but need not be limited to—

(a) a requirement to take a proportional, risk-based and differentiated approach to conducting transactions or business relationships with each category of PEP that may be defined; and

(b) specified categories of persons to be—

(i) included in, and

(ii) excluded from,

any definitions of PEPs.

(3) The Secretary of State may, by regulations, make provision about—

(a) the guidance issued, amended or reissued under subsection (1);

(b) arrangements for complaints about the treatment of individuals by regulated entities to be received, assessed and adjudicated by the FCA, where—

(i) a person was treated as though he or she was a PEP (and he or she was not),

(ii) a person who is a PEP was treated unreasonably in disregard of guidance under subsection (1), particularly in regard to specific elements required under subsection (2)(a), or

(iii) a person was refused a business relationship solely on the basis that he or she is a PEP,

(c) circumstances in which—

(i) compensation payments are to be required from, or

(ii) financial penalties are to be imposed on,

regulated entities where complaints under paragraph (b) are upheld.

(4) For the purposes of subsection (1), "relevant regulations" means regulations transposing into United Kingdom law measures that EU Member States are required to implement to combat money laundering (or subsequent regulations amending those regulations) that contain references to PEPs.

(5) The power to make regulations under subsection (3) is exercisable by statutory instrument which may only be made after a draft of any such instrument has been laid before, and approved by a resolution of, each House of Parliament."

Transformer vehicles

31 Transformer vehicles

(1) The Financial Services and Markets Act 2000 is amended as follows.

(2) After Part 17 insert—

"PART 17A

TRANSFORMER VEHICLES

284A Transformer vehicles

(1) In this section "transformer vehicle" means an undertaking ("A") which—

(a) is established for the purposes of carrying on the activities mentioned in subsection (2), or

(b) carries on those activities.

(2) The activities referred to in subsection (1) are—

(a) assuming risk from another undertaking ("B"), and

(b) fully funding A's exposure to that risk by issuing investments where the repayment rights of the investors are subordinated to A's obligations to B in respect of the risk.

(3) The Treasury may by regulations make provision for facilitating, and provision for regulating—

(a) the establishment and operation of transformer vehicles;

(b) the activities mentioned in subsection (2);

(c) the trading of investments issued by transformer vehicles.

(4) Regulations under subsection (3) may (amongst other things) make provision—

(a) for the incorporation and registration in the United Kingdom of bodies corporate;

(b) for a body incorporated by virtue of the regulations to take such form and name as may be determined in accordance with the regulations;

(c) as to the purposes for which such a body may exist and the investments which it may issue;

(d) as to the constitution, ownership, management and operation of such a body;

(e) for such a body to comprise different parts;

(f) for such parts to have legal personality distinct from that of the body;

(g) as to the holding and management of the assets and liabilities of such a body, including provision for the segregation of assets and liabilities relating to different risks;

(h) as to the powers, duties, rights and liabilities of such a body and of other persons, including—

(i) its directors and other officers;

(ii) its shareholders, and persons who hold the beneficial title to shares in it without holding the legal title;

(iii) its auditor;

(iv) any persons holding assets for it;

(v) any persons who act or purport to act on its behalf;

(i) as to the merger of one or more such bodies and the division of such a body;

(j) for the appointment and removal of an auditor for such a body;

(k) as to the winding up and dissolution of such a body;

(l) enabling the FCA or the PRA to apply to a court for an order removing or replacing any director of, or person holding assets for, such a body;

(m) for the carrying out of investigations by persons appointed by the FCA or the PRA.

(5) If regulations under subsection (3) make the provision mentioned in subsection (4)(e) references in subsection (4) to a body include its constituent parts.

(6) Regulations under subsection (3) may—

(a) impose criminal liability;

(b) confer functions on the FCA or the PRA (including the functions of making rules and giving directions);

(c) authorise the FCA or the PRA to require the Council of Lloyd's to exercise functions on its behalf (including functions conferred otherwise than by the regulations);

(d) confer jurisdiction on any court or on the Tribunal;

(e) provide for fees to be charged by the FCA or the PRA in connection with the carrying out of any of their functions under the regulations (including fees payable on a periodical basis);

(f) modify, exclude or apply (with or without modifications) any primary or subordinate legislation (including any provision of, or made under, this Act);

(g) make consequential amendments, repeals and revocations of any such legislation;

(h) modify or exclude any rule of law.

(7) Regulations under subsection (3) may make the provision mentioned in subsection (6)(c) only with the consent of the Council of Lloyd's.

(8) The provision that may be made by virtue of subsection (6)(f) includes provision extending or adapting any power to make subordinate legislation.

(9) Regulations under subsection (3) may provide that a reference in the regulations to, or to any provision of, legislation (including an EU instrument and legislation of a country or territory outside the United Kingdom) is to be construed as a reference to that legislation or that provision as amended from time to time.

(10) In this section—

"investment" includes any asset, right or interest;

"primary legislation" means an Act, an Act of the Scottish Parliament, a Measure or Act of the National Assembly for Wales, or Northern Ireland legislation;

"subordinate legislation" means an instrument made under primary legislation.

(11) If a statutory instrument containing regulations under this section would, apart from this subsection, be treated as a hybrid instrument for the purposes of the Standing Orders of either House of Parliament, it is to proceed in that House as if it were not a hybrid instrument."

(3) In section 429(2) (regulations subject to the affirmative procedure), after "262," insert "284A,".

Pensions

32 Pensions guidance

(1) Section 333A of the Financial Services and Markets Act 2000 (meaning of "pensions guidance" in Part 20A of that Act) is amended as follows.

(2) In subsection (2)—

(a) the words from "guidance", in the second place it occurs, to the end become paragraph (a);

(b) at the end of that paragraph insert ", and

(b) guidance given for the purpose of helping an individual who has a relevant interest in relation to a relevant annuity to make decisions in connection with transferring or otherwise dealing with the right to payments under that annuity."

(3) After subsection (2) insert—

"(2A) In subsection (2)(a)—

(a) references to a member, or a survivor of a member, of a pension scheme include a member, or a survivor of a member, of a pension scheme for which the PPF has assumed responsibility under Part 2 of the Pensions Act 2004 or Part 3 of the Pensions (Northern Ireland) Order 2005 (S.I. 2005/255 (N.I. 1)), but

(b) in relation to such a member or survivor, the reference to the flexible benefits that may be provided is to be read as a reference to the money purchase benefits (within the meaning of that Act or that Order) that may be provided by the PPF by virtue of sections 161 and 170 of that Act or articles 145 and 154 of that Order.

(2B) The Secretary of State may by regulations specify—

(a) the annuities that are relevant annuities for the purposes of subsection (2)(b), and

(b) the interests (which may include contingent interests) that are relevant interests for the purposes of that subsection."

(4) In subsection (3) after the definition of "pension scheme" insert—

"“PPF” means the Board of the Pension Protection Fund;".

33 Advice about transferring or otherwise dealing with annuity payments

(1) The Financial Services and Markets Act 2000 is amended as follows.

(2) After section 137FB insert—

"137FBA FCA general rules: advice about transferring or otherwise dealing with annuity payments

(1) The FCA must make general rules requiring specified authorised persons to check that an individual—

(a) who has a right to payments under a relevant annuity, and

(b) if the Treasury make regulations under subsection (3), who is not an exempt person by virtue of those regulations,

has received appropriate advice before transferring or otherwise dealing with the right to those payments.

(2) The reference in subsection (1) to a right to payments under a relevant annuity does not include a contingent right to such payments.

(3) The Treasury may by regulations provide that an individual whose financial circumstances meet criteria specified in the regulations is an exempt person for the purposes of subsection (1)(b).

(4) Regulations made under subsection (3) may (amongst other things) specify criteria based on the proportion of the individual's financial resources that is represented by the payments under the relevant annuity or the value of that annuity.

(5) The rules made by virtue of subsection (1) may include provision—

(a) about what specified authorised persons must do to check that an individual has received appropriate advice for the purposes of those rules;

(b) about when the check must be carried out.

(6) For the purposes of this section—

(a) "relevant annuity" means an annuity specified (by type, value or otherwise) as a relevant annuity in regulations made by the Treasury;

(b) "appropriate advice" means advice specified (by reference to the person giving the advice or otherwise) as appropriate advice in regulations made by the Treasury;

(c) "specified authorised person" means an authorised person of a description specified in rules made by virtue of subsection (1).

(7) If regulations under subsection (3) or (6)(a) make provision about the value of an annuity, the regulations may also make provision about the basis on which the value of an annuity is to be calculated."

(3) In section 138F(2) (notification of rules) after "137FB," insert "137FBA,".

(4) In section 138I (consultation by the FCA)—

(a) in subsection (6), after paragraph (aa) insert—

"(ab) section 137FBA;";

(b) in subsection (10)(a) after "137FB," insert "137FBA,".

(5) In section 429(2B) (regulations subject to affirmative procedure)—

(a) after paragraph (a) (inserted by section 22) insert—

"(b) provision made under section 137FBA(3);";

(b) the words from "provision made under section 410A," to the end become paragraph (c).

34 Independent advice on conversions and transfers of pension benefits: appointed representatives

(1) The Pension Schemes Act 2015 is amended as follows.

(2) In section 48(8) (independent advice in respect of conversions and transfers: Great Britain), in paragraph (a) of the definition of "authorised independent adviser", after "Secretary of State," insert "or is acting as an appointed representative (within the meaning given by section 39(2) of that Act) in relation to a regulated activity so specified,".

(3) In section 51(8) (independent advice in respect of conversions and transfers: Northern Ireland), in paragraph (a) of the definition of "authorised independent adviser", after "Northern Ireland," insert "or is acting as an appointed representative (within the meaning given by section 39(2) of that Act) in relation to a regulated activity so specified,".

(4) The Financial Services and Markets Act 2000 (Appointed Representatives) Regulations 2001 (S.I. 2001/1217) are amended as follows.

(5) In regulation 2(1) (descriptions of business for which appointed representatives are exempt) after sub-paragraph (cca) insert—

"(ccb) an activity of the kind specified by article 53E of that Order (advising on conversion or transfer of pension benefits);".

(6) In regulation 3 (requirements applying to contracts between authorised persons and appointed representatives) after paragraph (3G) insert—

"(3GA) A representative is also to be treated as representing other counterparties for the purposes of paragraph (1) where the representative gives advice (in circumstances constituting the carrying on of an activity of the kind specified by article 53E of that Order) on behalf of other counterparties."

(7) The amendments made by subsections (4) to (6) do not affect the power to make further subordinate legislation amending or revoking the amended regulations.

35 Early exit pension charges

(1) The Financial Services and Markets Act 2000 is amended as follows.

(2) After section 137FBA (as inserted by section 33) insert—

"137FBB FCA general rules: early exit pension charges

(1) The FCA must make general rules prohibiting authorised persons from—

(a) imposing specified early exit charges on members of relevant pension schemes, and

(b) including in relevant pension schemes provision for the imposition of specified early exit charges on members of such schemes.

(2) The rules must be made with a view to securing, so far as is reasonably possible, an appropriate degree of protection for members of relevant pension schemes against early exit charges being a deterrent on taking, converting or transferring benefits under the schemes.

(3) The rules may specify early exit charges by reference to charges of a specified class or description, or by reference to charges which exceed a specified amount.

(4) The rules made by virtue of subsection (1)(a) must prohibit the imposition of the charges after those rules come into force, whether the relevant pension scheme was established before or after those rules (or this section) came into force.

(5) In relation to a charge which is imposed, or provision for the imposition of a charge which is included in a pension scheme, in contravention of the rules, the rules may (amongst other things)—

(a) provide for the obligation to pay the charge to be unenforceable or unenforceable to a specified extent;

(b) provide for the recovery of amounts paid in respect of the charge;

(c) provide for the payment of compensation for any losses incurred as a result of paying amounts in respect of the charge.

(6) Subject to subsection (8) an early exit charge, in relation to a member of a pension scheme, is a charge which—

(a) is imposed under the scheme when a member who has reached normal minimum pension age takes the action mentioned in subsection (7), but

(b) is only imposed, or only imposed to that extent, if the member takes that action before the member's expected retirement date.

(7) The action is the member taking benefits under the scheme, converting benefits under the scheme into different benefits or transferring benefits under the scheme to another pension scheme.

(8) The Treasury may by regulations specify matters that are not to be treated as early exit charges for the purposes of this section.

(9) For the purposes of this section—

"charge", in relation to a member of a pension scheme, includes a reduction in the value of the member's benefits under the scheme;

"expected retirement date", in relation to a member of a pension scheme, means the date determined by, or in accordance with, the scheme as the date on which the member's benefits under the scheme are expected to be taken;

"normal minimum pension age" has the same meaning as in section 279(1) of the Finance Act 2004;

"relevant pension scheme" has the same meaning as in section 137FB;

and a reference to benefits includes all or any part of those benefits."

(3) In section 138E(3) (contravention of rules which may make transaction void or unenforceable)—

(a) omit the "or" at the end of paragraph (a);

(b) at the end of paragraph (b) insert "or

(c) rules made by the FCA under section 137FBB."

Information about resolution planning

36 Duty of Bank to provide information to Treasury

(1) The Financial Services Act 2012 is amended as follows.

(2) Before section 58 insert—

"57A Duty of Bank to provide information required by Treasury

(1) The Treasury may by notice in writing require the Bank of England to provide it with information specified, or of a description specified, in the notice.

(2) The information must be information which the Treasury consider is material to the Bank's assessment of the implications for public funds of a bank, building society, credit union or investment firm failing.

(3) The information must be provided before the end of such reasonable period as may be specified in the notice.

(4) The Bank's duty to provide information under this section does not apply to information which the Bank does not have in its possession.

(5) For the purposes of this section, the cases in which a bank, building society, credit union or investment firm ("the institution") is to be regarded as failing include those where—

(a) the institution enters insolvency,

(b) any of the stabilisation options in Part 1 of the Banking Act 2009 is achieved in relation to the institution, or

(c) the institution falls to be taken for the purposes of the Financial Services Compensation Scheme (within the meaning given by section 213 of FSMA 2000) to be unable, or likely to be unable, to satisfy claims against the institution.

(6) In subsection (5)(a) "insolvency" includes—

(a) bankruptcy;

(b) liquidation;

(c) bank insolvency;

(d) building society insolvency;

(e) investment bank insolvency;

(f) administration;

(g) bank administration;

(h) building society special administration;

(i) receivership;

(j) a composition between the institution and the institution's creditors;

(k) a scheme of arrangement of the institution's affairs.

(7) For the purposes of this section—

"bank" has the meaning given by section 2 of the Banking Act 2009,

"bank administration" has the same meaning as in that Act (see section 136 of that Act),

"bank insolvency" has the same meaning as in that Act (see section 90 of that Act),

"building society", "building society insolvency" and "building society special administration" have the same meaning as in the Building Societies Act 1986 (see section 119 of that Act),

"credit union" means a credit union as defined by section 31 of the Credit Unions Act 1979 or a credit union as defined by Article 2(2) of the Credit Unions (Northern Ireland) Order 1985,

"investment bank insolvency" means any procedure established by regulations under section 233 of the Banking Act 2009,

"investment firm" has the same meaning as in that Act (see section 258A of that Act),

"public funds" means the Consolidated Fund and any other account or source of money which cannot be drawn or spent other than by, or with the authority of, the Treasury,

and an event has implications for public funds if it would or might involve or lead to a need for the application of public funds.

57B Duty of Bank to inform Treasury about resolution plans

(1) This section applies in relation to—

(a) a resolution plan which includes one or more options for the exercise of a stabilisation power by the Bank of England in relation to an institution ("the institution"), and

(b) a group resolution plan which includes one or more options for the exercise of a stabilisation power by the Bank of England in relation to a group entity ("the entity").

(2) Unless otherwise directed under subsection (5), before adopting the plan the Bank must provide the Treasury with—

(a) a copy of the plan,

(b) the Bank's assessment of the systemic risk of the institution or the entity failing,

(c) the Bank's assessment of the implications for public funds—

(i) of the exercise by the Bank of a stabilisation power in relation to the institution or the entity in accordance with the option (or each of the options) for the exercise of such a power included in the plan, and

(ii) if the plan includes one or more options for the use of an insolvency or administration procedure in relation to the institution or the entity, of the use of such a procedure in accordance with that option (or each of those options), and

(d) any analysis considered by the Bank (whether or not prepared by the Bank) to be material in making the assessments mentioned in paragraph (c).

(3) Unless otherwise directed under subsection (5), the Bank must provide the Treasury with details of—

(a) any material changes to the plan, before those changes are adopted,

(b) any material changes to the Bank's assessments of the matters mentioned in subsection (2)(b) or (c), and

(c) any further analysis considered by the Bank (whether or not prepared by the Bank) to be material to revising the assessments mentioned in subsection (2)(c).

(4) Where reasonably practicable the Bank must comply with subsections (2) and (3) before the Bank exercises any of its powers under section 3A of the Banking Act 2009 in relation to the institution or the entity.

(5) The Treasury may by notice in writing—

(a) direct the Bank not to provide it under this section with information in relation to institutions or entities specified, or of a description specified, in the notice;

(b) revoke a direction given under paragraph (a).

(6) Where a direction given under subsection (5)(a) is revoked—

(a) the Bank must provide the Treasury with the matters listed in subsection (2)(a) to (d) in relation to the institutions or entities to which the direction related as soon as reasonably practicable after the date of the revocation, and

(b) subsection (3) applies in relation to those institutions or entities,

but this is subject to any further direction under subsection (5)(a).

(7) For the purposes of this section—

"failing" has the same meaning as in section 57A,

"insolvency or administration procedure" means—

(a) bank insolvency,

(b) building society insolvency,

(c) investment bank insolvency,

(d) bank administration, or

(e) building society special administration,

(and those terms have the same meaning as in section 57A);

"public funds" has the same meaning as in section 57A,

"systemic risk" means risk to the stability of the financial system in the United Kingdom or in other EEA states,

and action has implications for public funds if it would or might involve or lead to a need for the application of public funds."

(3) In section 65 (memorandum of understanding)—

(a) in subsection (1), after "in relation to" insert—

"(a) the sharing of information by the Bank about any proposals to include in a resolution plan or a group resolution plan an option for the exercise of a stabilisation power by the Bank in relation to an institution or group entity;

(b)";

(b) in subsection (2), at the beginning insert "For the purposes of subsection (1) (b),";

(c) in the heading, after "understanding:" insert "resolution planning and".

(4) In section 67 (interpretation), after subsection (5) insert—

"(6) Group entity" has the same meaning as in the Bank Recovery and Resolution (No. 2) Order 2014 (S.I. 2014/3348).

(7) "Group resolution plan" means a group resolution plan drawn up by the Bank under Part 5 of that Order.

(8) "Resolution plan" means a resolution plan drawn up by the Bank under Part 5 of that Order.

(9) "Stabilisation power" has the same meaning as in section 1(4) of the Banking Act 2009."

Financial Services and Markets Act 2000 consequential amendments

37 Financial Services and Markets Act 2000 (Consequential Amendments and Repeals) Order 2001

(1) The revocation of the Financial Services and Markets Act 2000 (Consequential Amendments and Repeals) Order 2001 (S.I. 2001/3649) by the National Savings Regulations 2015 (S.I. 2015/623) is to be treated as never having had effect.

(2) Accordingly, in the Schedule to those regulations, omit the entry for that order.

PART 3

MISCELLANEOUS AND GENERAL

Banknotes in Scotland and Northern Ireland

38 Banks authorised to issue banknotes in Scotland and Northern Ireland

(1) The Banking Act 2009 is amended as follows.

(2) In section 207(b) (overview of Part 6) for the words from "banks" to the end substitute "authorised banks (see section 210)."

(3) In section 210 (authorised bank)—

(a) the words from "a bank" to the end become paragraph (a);

(b) at the end of that paragraph insert "(unless by virtue of regulations under section 214A it is no longer an authorised bank for the purposes of this Part), or";

(c) after that paragraph insert—

"(b) a bank which is designated as an authorised bank for the purposes of this Part by regulations under section 214A(1)(a)."

(4) In section 213 (saving for existing issuers)—

(a) the existing text becomes subsection (1);

(b) in that subsection, after "bank" insert "within section 210(a)";

(c) after that subsection insert—

"(2) An authorised bank within section 210(b) may issue banknotes, but only—

(a) in accordance with the provisions of this Part, and

(b) in the part of the United Kingdom which is specified in relation to the bank in regulations under section 214A(1)(b).";

(d) for the heading substitute "Authorisation to issue banknotes".

(5) After section 214 insert—

"214A Power to designate banks as "authorised banks"

(1) The Treasury may by regulations—

(a) specify a bank which on and after the designation date is designated as an authorised bank for the purposes of this Part,

(b) specify a part of the United Kingdom in which the bank may issue banknotes, and

(c) make provision about how the bank is to be identified on those banknotes.

(2) Regulations under subsection (1)—

(a) may only specify under paragraph (a) a bank (the newly authorised bank) which is in the same group as an authorised bank (the previously authorised bank) which has the right to rely on section 213;

(b) may only specify under paragraph (b) the part of the United Kingdom in which the previously authorised bank is authorised to issue banknotes;

(c) must procure that on and after the designation date the previously authorised bank is no longer an authorised bank for the purposes of this Part by—

(i) in the case of a previously authorised bank within section 210(a), providing that it is no longer an authorised bank for the purposes of this Part;

(ii) in the case of a previously authorised bank within section 210(b), revoking its designation;

(d) must provide for the newly authorised bank to be treated as having issued any banknotes in circulation which were issued by the previously authorised bank;

(e) must provide for the transfer of any rights or liabilities in relation to those banknotes to the newly authorised bank from the previously authorised bank;

(f) may provide for anything done by or in relation to the previously authorised bank in connection with those banknotes to be treated as having been done by or in relation to the newly authorised bank for the purposes specified in the regulations;

(g) may make further provision about banknotes issued by the previously authorised bank;

(h) may make provision about banknotes held by or on behalf of the previously authorised bank which are not in circulation.

(3) The reference in subsection (2)(d) and (g) to banknotes issued by the previously authorised bank includes a reference to banknotes which are to be treated as having been issued by that bank as a result of regulations made under subsection (1) (or any other enactment).

(4) Regulations under subsection (1) must—

(a) specify a date as the designation date, or

(b) if no such date is specified, make provision for the designation date to be determined by the Treasury and published by the Treasury before the designation date in the appropriate Gazettes.

(5) The appropriate Gazettes are the London Gazette and—

(a) if the part of the United Kingdom specified under subsection (1)(b) is Scotland, the Edinburgh Gazette;

(b) if the part of the United Kingdom specified under subsection (1)(b) is Northern Ireland, the Belfast Gazette.

(6) Before specifying a bank under subsection (1)(a) the Treasury must obtain the consent of the Bank of England.

(7) The Bank of England must prepare and publish a statement of the matters which it intends to take into account in deciding whether to give its consent.

(8) The power to make regulations under this section—

(a) is exercisable by statutory instrument;

(b) includes a power to make transitory or saving provision;

(c) includes a power to apply (with or without modifications) or disapply any provision of an Act or subordinate legislation whenever passed or made.

(9) A statutory instrument containing regulations under this section may not be made unless a draft of the instrument has been laid before and approved by a resolution of each House of Parliament.

(10) For the purposes of this section—

"bank" has the same meaning as in Part 1 (see section 2),

"designation date" in relation to regulations under subsection (1) means the date specified or determined, as the case may be, in accordance with subsection (4),

"group" has the meaning given by section 421 of the Financial Services and Markets Act 2000, and

a banknote is in circulation from the time that it is issued by an authorised bank until the time that it is returned to the bank (or a bank which is treated as having issued it as a result of regulations made under subsection (1) or any other enactment)."

(6) In section 259(3) (statutory instruments), in Part 6 of the Table, before the entry relating to section 215 insert—

"214A	Issuers of banknotes: Scotland and Northern Ireland	Draft affirmative resolution"

General

39 Consequential provision

(1) The Treasury or the Secretary of State may by regulations make the provision in subsection (2) in consequence of any provision made by or under this Act.

(2) The provision referred to in subsection (1) is provision amending, repealing, revoking or applying with modifications any provision of primary or secondary legislation to which this section applies.

(3) This section applies to primary and secondary legislation passed or made—

(a) before the passing of this Act, or

(b) on or before the last day of the session in which this Act is passed.

(4) Regulations under this section—

(a) may make saving, transitory or transitional provision;

(b) may make different provision for different purposes.

(5) The power to make regulations under this section is exercisable by statutory instrument.

(6) A statutory instrument containing regulations under this section—

(a) if it contains (whether alone or with other provision) provision which amends or repeals any provision of primary legislation, may not be made unless a draft of the instrument has been laid before, and approved by a resolution of, each House of Parliament, and

(b) otherwise, is subject to annulment in pursuance of a resolution of either House of Parliament.

(7) In this section—

"primary legislation" means an Act, an Act of the Scottish Parliament, a Measure or Act of the National Assembly for Wales, or Northern Ireland legislation;

"secondary legislation" means an instrument made under primary legislation.

40 Extent

(1) Subject to subsection (2) this Act extends to England and Wales, Scotland and Northern Ireland.

(2) An amendment or repeal made by this Act has the same extent as the provision amended or repealed.

41 Commencement

(1) The following provisions come into force on the day on which this Act is passed—

(a) section 31;

(b) section 37;

(c) sections 39 to 42.

(2) Section 32 comes into force on such day as the Secretary of State may by regulations appoint.

(3) The other provisions of this Act come into force on such day as the Treasury may by regulations appoint.

(4) The Treasury or the Secretary of State may by regulations make saving, transitory or transitional provision in connection with the coming into force of any provision made by or under this Act.

(5) Regulations under this section may make different provision for different purposes.

(6) The power to make regulations under this section is exercisable by statutory instrument.

42 Short title

This Act may be cited as the Bank of England and Financial Services Act 2016.

SCHEDULES

SCHEDULE 1

Section 13

PRUDENTIAL REGULATION COMMITTEE

"SCHEDULE 6A

Section 30A

PRUDENTIAL REGULATION COMMITTEE

1 Interpretation

1 In this Schedule—

"chief executive for prudential regulation" means the Deputy Governor for prudential regulation, acting in his or her capacity as a member of the Committee or by virtue of a delegation under paragraph 17;

"the Committee" means the Prudential Regulation Committee;

"prudential regulation strategy" means the strategy determined by the Prudential Regulation Authority under section 2E of the Financial Services and Markets Act 2000.

2 Appointment of members by Chancellor

2 Before appointing a person as a member of the Committee under section 30A(2)(g), the Chancellor of the Exchequer must—

(a) be satisfied that the person has knowledge or experience which is likely to be relevant to the Committee's functions, and

(b) consider whether the person has any financial or other interests that could substantially affect the functions as member that it would be proper for the person to discharge.

3 Term of office of appointed members

3 (1) Appointment as a member of the Committee under section 30A(2)(f) or (g) is to be for a period of 3 years, but this is subject to sub-paragraph (2) and to paragraph 5.

(2) Initially some appointments may be for shorter and different periods so as to secure that appointments expire at different times.

4 (1) A person may not be appointed as a member of the Committee under section 30A(2)(g) more than twice.

(2) For this purpose an appointment which by virtue of paragraph 3(2) is for a period of less than 3 years is to be disregarded.

5 (1) If it appears to the Chancellor of the Exchequer that in the circumstances it is desirable to do so, the Chancellor may, before the end of the term for which a person is appointed as a member of the Committee under section 30A(2)(g), extend the

person's term of office on one occasion for a specified period of not more than 6 months.

(2) The term being extended may be the person's first or second term or, in a case where paragraph 4(2) allows a third term, the person's third term.

(3) If a person whose first term of office is extended is subsequently re-appointed under section 30A(2)(g)—

(a) the length of the second term is to be reduced by a period equal to the extension of the first term, but

(b) the second term may itself be extended under sub-paragraph (1).

(4) In a case where a person's second term of office is extended and paragraph 4(2) allows a third term, sub-paragraph (3) is to be read as if the references to first and second terms were references to second and third terms respectively.

6 (1) A person appointed under section 30A(2)(f) or (g) may resign the office by written notice to the Bank.

(2) Where the notice relates to a person appointed under section 30A(2)(g) the Bank must give a copy of the notice to the Treasury.

7 Terms and conditions of appointment

7 (1) The terms on which a person is appointed as a member of the Committee under section 30A(2)(g) must be such as—

(a) to secure that the member is not subject to direction by the Bank or the Treasury,

(b) to require the member not to act in accordance with the directions of any other person, and

(c) to prohibit the member from acquiring any financial or other interests that have a material effect on the extent of the functions as member that it would be proper for the member to discharge.

(2) The terms and conditions on which a person holds office as a member of the Committee appointed under section 30A(2)(g) are to be determined by the court of directors.

8 Qualification for appointment

8 (1) The following persons are disqualified for appointment under section 30A(2)(f) or (g)—

(a) a minister of the Crown;

(b) a person serving in a government department in employment in respect of which remuneration is paid out of money provided by Parliament.

(2) The following persons are disqualified for appointment under section 30A(2)(g)—

(a) a member of the Financial Policy Committee of the Bank appointed under section 9B(1)(e);

(b) a member of the Monetary Policy Committee of the Bank appointed under section 13(2)(c).

9 Removal of appointed members

9 (1) A person appointed under section 30A(2)(f) or (g) vacates office on becoming a person to whom paragraph 8(1) applies.

(2) The court of directors of the Bank may, with the consent of the Chancellor of the Exchequer, remove a member appointed under section 30A(2)(f) or (g) ("M") if it is satisfied—

(a) that M has been absent from 3 or more meetings of the Prudential Regulation Committee without the Committee's consent,

(b) that M has become bankrupt, that a debt relief order (under Part 7A of the Insolvency Act 1986) has been made in respect of M, that M's estate has been sequestrated or that M has made an arrangement with or granted a trust deed for M's creditors, or

(c) that M is unable or unfit to discharge M's functions as a member.

(3) The court of directors may, with the consent of the Chancellor of the Exchequer, also remove a member appointed under section 30A(2)(g) ("M") if it is satisfied that in all the circumstances M's financial or other interests are such as substantially to affect the functions as member which it would be proper for M to discharge.

10 Decision making

10 (1) Decisions of the Committee must be taken either—

(a) at a meeting of the Committee in accordance with paragraphs 11 to 15, or

(b) in writing in accordance with paragraph 16.

(2) Subject to paragraphs 11 to 16, the Committee is to determine its own procedure.

11 Meetings

11 The Governor of the Bank or any Deputy Governor of the Bank who is a member of the Committee may summon a meeting at any time by giving such notice as the person giving the notice thinks the circumstances require.

12 (1) At a meeting of the Committee, the proceedings are to be regulated as follows.

(2) The quorum is to be determined by the Committee, but it must be not less than 3 and of those 3—

(a) one must be the Governor of the Bank, the Bank's Deputy Governor for financial stability or the Bank's Deputy Governor for markets and banking,

(b) unless both the Governor and the Bank's Deputy Governor for financial stability are present, one must be the Bank's Deputy Governor for prudential regulation, and

(c) one must be a member appointed under section 30A(2)(g).

(3) The chair is to be taken by the Governor of the Bank or, if the Governor is not present, by the Deputy Governor for financial stability or the Deputy Governor for markets and banking.

(4) The person chairing the meeting must seek to ensure that decisions of the Committee are reached by consensus wherever possible.

(5) Where that person forms the opinion that consensus cannot be reached, a decision is to be taken by a vote of all those members present at the meeting (subject to paragraphs 13 and 14).

(6) In the event of a tie, the person chairing the meeting is to have a second casting vote.

13 The chief executive of the Financial Conduct Authority must not take part in any discussion by or decision of the Committee which relates to—

(a) the exercise of any functions of the Prudential Regulation Authority in relation to a particular person, or

(b) a decision not to exercise those functions.

14 (1) If a member of the Committee ("M") has any direct or indirect interest (including any reasonably likely future interest) in any dealing or business which falls to be considered by the Committee—

(a) M must disclose that interest to the Committee when it considers the dealing or business, and

(b) the Committee must decide whether M is to be permitted to participate in any proceedings of the Committee relating to any question arising from its consideration of the dealing or business, and if so to what extent and subject to what conditions (if any).

(2) The Bank must issue and maintain a code of practice describing how members of the Committee and the Committee are to comply with sub-paragraph (1).

(3) The Bank may at any time revise or replace the code.

(4) Before issuing, revising or replacing the code, the Bank must consult the Treasury.

(5) The Bank must publish the current version of the code in whatever manner it sees fit.

(6) The Committee must comply with the code when taking decisions under sub-paragraph (1)(b).

15 (1) The Committee may determine circumstances in which a member who is not present at, but is in communication with, a meeting is to be treated as present at it for the purposes of paragraph 12.

(2) The Committee may invite other persons to attend, or to attend and speak at, any meeting of the Committee.

16 Decisions otherwise than at meetings

16 (1) The Committee may take a decision on a matter without a meeting if—

(a) a majority of eligible members indicate in writing their agreement to the decision,

(b) the eligible members who indicate in writing their agreement to the decision would have constituted a quorum at a meeting of the Committee, and

(c) any other requirements determined by the Committee are met.

(2) "Eligible members" are members of the Committee who would have been entitled to vote on the matter if the matter had been proposed for decision at a meeting of the Committee.

17 Delegation of functions

17 (1) The Committee may delegate such of its functions as it thinks fit to—

(a) a member of the Committee,

(b) a sub-committee of the Committee consisting of—

(i) members of the Committee, or

(ii) one or more members of the Committee and one or more officers, employees or agents of the Bank,

(c) an officer, employee or agent of the Bank, or

(d) a committee consisting of officers, employees or agents of the Bank.

This is subject to sub-paragraphs (2) and (9).

(2) The Committee must delegate to the chief executive for prudential regulation the following functions—

(a) preparing for consideration by the Committee drafts of a prudential regulation strategy and any proposed revisions to that strategy;

(b) preparing for consideration by the Committee drafts of the annual budget required by paragraph 18 and any proposed variations of that budget;

(c) the day to day management of the Bank's functions as the Prudential Regulation Authority;

(d) the day to day implementation of the prudential regulation strategy.

This is subject to sub-paragraph (9).

(3) A delegation under sub-paragraph (2)—

(a) must identify any decisions (within sub-paragraph (9) or otherwise) that are not included in the delegation;

(b) may be on such terms and subject to such conditions as the Committee thinks fit.

(4) Those terms and conditions—

(a) may include provision about the manner of the exercise of the delegated functions;

(b) may be revised by the Committee from time to time.

(5) Sub-paragraph (2) does not apply in the event of a vacancy in the office of Deputy Governor for prudential regulation.

(6) The Bank must publish a statement setting out—

(a) the functions which the Committee has delegated to the chief executive for prudential regulation,

(b) the terms and conditions on which each delegation is made, and

(c) any decisions (within sub-paragraph (9) or otherwise) that are not included in the delegations.

(7) If there is a material change to any of those matters, the Bank must publish a revised statement.

(8) The requirement to delegate the functions mentioned in sub-paragraph (2) to the chief executive for prudential regulation does not prevent further delegation of those functions by the chief executive.

(9) The Committee may not delegate the following functions—

(a) reporting to the Chancellor of the Exchequer under paragraph 19;
(b) making rules under the Financial Services and Markets Act 2000;
(c) determining, reviewing and revising the prudential regulation strategy under section 2E of that Act;
(d) giving and reviewing guidance under section 2I of that Act;
(e) giving and revoking directions under section 3I, 3J, 3M, 316 or 318 of that Act;
(f) issuing statements under section 63ZD, 63C, 69, 142V, 192H, 192N, 210 or 345D of that Act;
(g) issuing statements under section 80 of the Financial Services Act 2012.

18 Prudential regulation budget

18 (1) The Committee must, with the approval of the court of directors, for each of the Bank's financial years adopt an annual budget for the Bank's functions as the Prudential Regulation Authority.

(2) The budget must be adopted before the start of the financial year to which it relates.

(3) The Committee may, with the approval of the court of directors, vary the budget for a financial year at any time after its adoption.

(4) The Bank must publish each budget, and each variation of a budget, in whatever way it thinks appropriate.

19 Annual reports

19 At least once a year the Committee must make a report to the Chancellor of the Exchequer on—

(a) the adequacy of the resources allocated, in the period to which the report relates, to the Bank's functions as the Prudential Regulation Authority, and
(b) the extent to which the exercise of the Bank's functions as the Prudential Regulation Authority is independent of the exercise of its other functions."

SCHEDULE 2

Section 16

AMENDMENTS RELATING TO PART 1

PART 1

BANK OF ENGLAND ACT 1998

1 The Bank of England Act 1998 is amended as follows.

2 In section 2 (functions of court of directors), for subsection (5) substitute—

"(5) Subsections (2) to (4) are subject to—

(a) section 2A (Financial Stability Objective);
(b) section 11 (objectives in relation to monetary policy);

(c) Part 1A of the Financial Services and Markets Act 2000 (objectives and strategy of the Prudential Regulation Authority)."

3 In section 2A(2) (financial stability objective) for ", the Financial Conduct Authority and the Prudential Regulation Authority)" substitute "and the Financial Conduct Authority)".

4 (1) Section 3A (oversight functions) is amended as follows.

(2) In subsection (2)(a)—

(a) in sub-paragraph (i), after "Act" insert ", the objectives specified in relation to the Prudential Regulation Authority in Part 1A of the Financial Services and Markets Act 2000";

(b) omit the "and" at the end of sub-paragraph (ii);

(c) for sub-paragraph (iii) substitute—

"(iii) the Bank's strategy determined under section 2,

(iv) the Bank's financial stability strategy determined under section 9A, and

(v) the strategy of the Prudential Regulation Authority determined under section 2E of the Financial Services and Markets Act 2000;".

(3) In subsection (4) omit paragraphs (c) to (h).

5 (1) Section 3C (reviews) is amended as follows.

(2) In subsection (1)—

(a) after "of its" insert "oversight";

(b) for "Oversight Committee" substitute "court of directors";

(c) in paragraphs (a) and (b) for "Committee" substitute "court of directors".

(3) In subsection (3)(a) for "by the Committee in the discharge of any of its" substitute "in relation to the discharge of any of the court's".

(4) Omit subsection (4).

(5) In subsection (5) for "the Committee must have regard" substitute "regard must be had".

6 In section 3D(1) (publication of reports of performance reviews) for "Oversight Committee" substitute "court of directors".

7 In section 3E(2) (recommendations resulting from review) for "Oversight Committee" substitute "court of directors".

8 (1) Section 3F (oversight: further provisions) is amended as follows.

(2) In subsection (1)—

(a) for "Oversight Committee" substitute "court of directors";

(b) after "of its" insert "oversight";

(c) for "or the Monetary Policy Committee" substitute ", the Monetary Policy Committee or the Prudential Regulation Committee".

(3) In subsection (2)—

(a) for "Oversight Committee" substitute "court of directors";

(b) for "or the Monetary Policy Committee" substitute ", the Monetary Policy Committee or the Prudential Regulation Committee for the purposes of exercising its oversight functions".

(4) After subsection (2) insert—

"(2A) But a member of the court of directors who has any direct or indirect interest (including any reasonably likely future interest) in any dealing or business which falls to be considered by the Prudential Regulation Committee may not, under the powers conferred by this section—

(a) obtain access to any documents relating to the dealing or business, or

(b) attend any proceedings of the Prudential Regulation Committee relating to any question arising from its consideration of the dealing or business."

(5) In subsection (3)—

(a) in paragraph (a)—

(i) after "Policy Committee" insert ", the Monetary Policy Committee or the Prudential Regulation Committee";

(ii) for "Oversight Committee" substitute "court of directors";

(b) omit the "or" at the end of paragraph (b);

(c) at the end of paragraph (c) insert ", or

(d) the powers of the Prudential Regulation Committee under paragraph 15(2) of Schedule 6A."

(6) In the heading, for "Committee" substitute "functions".

9 (1) Section 4 (annual report by the Bank) is amended as follows.

(2) For subsection (2)(a) substitute—

"(a) a report by the court of directors on the matters which it reviews, monitors or otherwise considers in the performance of its oversight functions (as defined by section 3A(2)),".

(3) In subsection (2)(b)—

(a) for "statement" substitute "statements";

(b) after "7(2)" insert "and (2A)";

(c) for "it" substitute "them".

(4) Omit subsection (3).

(5) After subsection (6) insert—

"(7) The Chancellor may comply with subsection (6) by laying a document containing a report under this section together with a report by the Prudential Regulation Authority under paragraph 19 of Schedule 1ZB to the Financial Services and Markets Act 2000."

10 Omit section 7A(9)(a) (definition of "qualifying company").

11 In section 9B(4) (Financial Policy Committee) for "Oversight Committee" substitute "court of directors of the Bank".

12 In section 9O (FPC recommendations within the Bank), after subsection (4) insert—

"(5) Recommendations by the Committee to the PRA are to be made under section 9Q (and not under this section)."

13 (1) Section 9Y (directions requiring information or documents) is amended as follows.

(2) In subsection (2) for "or the PRA ("the regulator") requiring the regulator" substitute "requiring it".

(3) In subsection (3) for "regulator", in each place it occurs, substitute "FCA".

(4) In subsection (4) omit—

(a) the "and" at the end of paragraph (a);

(b) paragraph (b).

(5) In the italic heading before section 9Y, omit "or PRA".

14 (1) Section 9Z (further provisions about directions under section 9Y) is amended as follows.

(2) In subsection (2)—

(a) omit "or the PRA ("the regulator")";

(b) for "regulator", in the second place it occurs, substitute "FCA".

(3) In subsection (4), for "regulator to which it is given" substitute "FCA".

15 In section 14 (publications of statements about decisions)—

(a) in subsection (1) after "As soon as" insert "reasonably";

(b) in subsection (5) after "As soon as" insert "reasonably".

16 (1) Section 16 (functions of Oversight Committee) is amended as follows.

(2) In subsection (1) for "Oversight Committee" substitute "court of directors of the Bank".

(3) In subsection (2) for "the function of the Oversight Committee" substitute "the court's function".

(4) In the heading, for "Oversight Committee" substitute "court of directors".

17 In section 18(6) (reports) after "as soon as" insert "reasonably".

18 In section 40(2) (orders) after "under—" insert—

"section 1A(1),".

19 (1) Schedule 1 (court of directors) is amended as follows.

(2) In paragraph 8(2) for "Chief Executive of the Prudential Regulation Authority" substitute "chief executive for prudential regulation (see Schedule 6A)".

(3) In paragraph 11(1), after paragraph (c) insert—

"(d) a committee consisting of officers, employees or agents of the Bank."

20 (1) Schedule 2A (Financial Policy Committee) is amended as follows.

(2) In paragraph 5 for "Oversight Committee" substitute "court of directors of the Bank".

(3) In paragraph 6 for sub-paragraph (2) substitute—

"(2) The following persons are disqualified for appointment under section 9B(1)(e)—

(a) a member of the Monetary Policy Committee of the Bank appointed under section 13(2)(c);

(b) a member of the Prudential Regulation Committee of the Bank appointed under section 30A(2)(g)."

(4) In paragraph 9—

(a) in sub-paragraph (1) for "Oversight Committee" substitute "court of directors of the Bank";

(b) in sub-paragraph (2) for "Oversight Committee" substitute "court of directors".

(5) In paragraph 11—

(a) in sub-paragraph (2)(b) for "either" substitute "one";

(b) omit sub-paragraph (8).

(6) In paragraph 14—

(a) the existing text becomes sub-paragraph (1);

(b) after that sub-paragraph insert—

"(2) The Bank must issue and maintain a code of practice describing how members of the Committee and the Committee are to comply with sub-paragraph (1).

(3) The Bank may at any time revise or replace the code.

(4) Before issuing, revising or replacing the code, the Bank must consult the Treasury.

(5) The Bank must publish the current version of the code in whatever manner it sees fit.

(6) The Committee must comply with the code when taking decisions under sub-paragraph (1)(b)."

(7) After paragraph 14 insert—

"15 Decisions otherwise than at meetings

15 (1) The Committee may take a decision on a matter without a meeting if—

(a) a majority of eligible members indicate in writing their agreement to the decision,

(b) the eligible members who indicate in writing their agreement to the decision would have constituted a quorum at a meeting of the Committee, and

(c) any other requirements determined by the Committee are met.

(2) "Eligible members" are members of the Committee who would have been entitled to vote on the matter if the matter had been proposed for decision at a meeting of the Committee.

16 Power to determine own procedure

16 Subject to paragraphs 11, 14 and 15, the Committee is to determine its own procedure."

21 (1) Schedule 3 (Monetary Policy Committee) is amended as follows.

(2) In paragraph 4(2) for "Oversight Committee" substitute "court of directors of the Bank".

(3) For paragraph 5A substitute—

"5A The following persons are disqualified for appointment under section 13(2)(c)—

(a) a member of the Financial Policy Committee of the Bank appointed under section 9B(1)(e);

(b) a member of the Prudential Regulation Committee of the Bank appointed under section 30A(2)(g)."

(4) In paragraph 8—

(a) for "have executive responsibility" substitute "carry out monetary policy analysis";

(b) omit the words from "for" to the end.

(5) In paragraph 9(1)—

(a) for "Oversight Committee" substitute "court of directors of the Bank";

(b) in paragraph (a) for "meetings of the Monetary Policy Committee for more than 3 months" substitute "3 or more meetings of the Monetary Policy Committee".

(6) After paragraph 9(1) insert—

"(1A) The court of directors may, with the consent of the Chancellor of the Exchequer, also remove a member appointed under section 13(2)(c) if it is satisfied that in all the circumstances his financial or other interests are such as substantially to affect the functions as member which it would be proper for him to discharge."

(7) In paragraph 14 for "submit a monthly" substitute ", at least 8 times in each calendar year, submit a".

22 (1) Schedule 7 (restriction on disclosure of information) is amended as follows.

(2) In paragraph 2(1)—

(a) omit the "or" at the end of sub-paragraph (b);

(b) at the end of sub-paragraph (c) insert "or

(d) its functions as the Prudential Regulation Authority."

(3) In paragraph 3(1), in column 1 of the table, in the entry for the Financial Conduct Authority or the Prudential Regulation Authority omit "or the Prudential Regulation Authority".

PART 2

OTHER ACTS

Bank of England Act 1946 (c. 27)

23 In section 4(1) of the Bank of England Act 1946 (power of Treasury to give directions to the Bank)—

(a) the words "monetary policy" become paragraph (a);

(b) after that paragraph insert—

"(b) the exercise by the Bank of its functions as the Prudential Regulation Authority (see section 2A of the Financial Services and Markets Act 2000)."

House of Commons Disqualification Act 1975 (c. 24)

24 In Part 3 of Schedule 1 to the House of Commons Disqualification Act 1975 (other disqualifying offices)—

(a) omit "Member of the governing body of the Prudential Regulation Authority;";

(b) at the appropriate place insert—

"Member of the Prudential Regulation Committee of the Bank of England appointed under section 30A(2)(f) or (g) of the Bank of England Act 1998".

Northern Ireland Assembly Disqualification Act 1975 (c. 25)

25 In Part 3 of Schedule 1 to the Northern Ireland Assembly Disqualification Act 1975 (other disqualifying offices)—

(a) omit "Member of the governing body of the Prudential Regulation Authority;";

(b) at the appropriate place insert—

"Member of the Prudential Regulation Committee of the Bank of England appointed under section 30A(2)(f) or (g) of the Bank of England Act 1998".

Financial Services and Markets Act 2000 (c. 8)

26 The Financial Services and Markets Act 2000 is amended as follows.

27 Omit section 2O (independent reviews of PRA).

28 Omit section 2P (right to obtain documents etc for purposes of section 2O).

29 In section 3C (duty to follow principles of good governance), for "each regulator" substitute "the FCA".

30 (1) Section 3Q (co-operation by FCA and PRA with Bank of England) is amended as follows.

(2) In the heading, omit "and PRA".

(3) In subsection (1), for "Each regulator" substitute "The FCA".

(4) In subsection (2), for "regulator" substitute "FCA".

31 In section 3R(2) (arrangements for provision of services by and to Bank of England) —

(a) for "Either regulator" substitute "The FCA";

(b) in paragraphs (a) and (b), for "regulator" substitute "FCA".

32 After section 3S insert—

"Interpretation

3T Interpretation

3T Interpretation

In this Part "enactment" includes—

(a) an enactment contained in subordinate legislation within the meaning of the Interpretation Act 1978;

(b) an enactment contained in, or in an instrument made under, an Act of the Scottish Parliament;

(c) an enactment contained in, or in an instrument made under, a Measure or Act of the National Assembly for Wales;

(d) an enactment contained in, or in an instrument made under, Northern Ireland legislation."

33 (1) Section 137J (rules about recovery plans) is amended as follows.

(2) In subsection (1), for paragraphs (a) and (b) substitute "the Treasury".

(3) After subsection (1) insert—

"(1A) The FCA must also consult the Bank of England."

34 (1) Section 137K (rules about resolution packs) is amended as follows.

(2) In subsection (1), for paragraphs (a) and (b) substitute "the Treasury".

(3) After subsection (1) insert—

"(1A) The FCA must also consult the Bank of England."

35 (1) Section 138F (notification of rules) is amended as follows.

(2) In subsection (1), for paragraphs (a) and (b) substitute "to the Treasury".

(3) After subsection (1) insert—

"(1A) The FCA must also give written notice to the Bank of England."

(4) In subsection (2) for "(1)(b)" substitute "(1A)".

36 (1) Section 165 (regulators' power to require information: authorised persons etc) is amended as follows.

(2) In subsection (4)—

(a) the words from "information" to the end become paragraph (a);

(b) at the end of that paragraph (a) insert ", and

(b) in relation to the exercise by the PRA of the powers conferred by subsections (1) and (3), information and documents reasonably required by the Bank of England in connection with the exercise by the Bank of its functions in pursuance of its financial stability objective."

(3) After subsection (8) insert—

"(8A) Financial stability objective" means the objective set out in section 2A of the Bank of England Act 1998."

37 (1) Section 165A (PRA's power to require information: financial stability) is amended as follows.

(2) In subsection (3)—

(a) the words from "information" to the end become paragraph (a);

(b) at the end of that paragraph (a) insert ", and

(b) information and documents reasonably required by the Bank of England in connection with the exercise by the Bank of its functions in pursuance of its financial stability objective."

(3) After subsection (7) insert—

"(7A) Financial stability objective" means the objective set out in section 2A of the Bank of England Act 1998."

38 In section 187A(5A) (assessment: consultation by PRA with FCA) for "has been directed by the Bank of England under section 189(1A)" substitute "is required by section 189(1ZB)".

39 (1) Section 189 (assessment procedure) is amended as follows.

(2) In subsection (1A), for "But where" substitute "Where the appropriate regulator is the FCA and".

(3) After subsection (1A) insert—

"(1ZB) Where the appropriate regulator is the PRA and—

(a) the section 178 notice relates to an acquisition or increase of control over a credit institution, investment firm or banking group company, and

(b) the credit institution, investment firm or banking group company is one in relation to which the Bank of England is exercising its functions under sections 6A to 6C of the Banking Act 2009 or the special resolution regime under Part 1 of that Act,

the PRA must act under this Part in a timely manner, and shorten the assessment period so far as reasonably practicable."

(4) In subsection (1B)—

(a) for "subsection (1A)" substitute "subsections (1A) and (1ZB)";

(b) omit the definition of "bank";

(c) in the definition of "banking group company" for "that Act" substitute "the Banking Act 2009".

40 In section 190(1A) (requests for further information), after "189(1A)" insert "or section 189(1ZB) applies".

41 In section 192F(3) (consultation between regulators)—

(a) for "either regulator" substitute "the FCA";

(b) for "the regulator" substitute "it".

42 In section 192I(1)(a) (statement of policy relating to directions) after "regulator and" insert ", where the issuing regulator is the FCA,".

43 In section 285A(3)(a) (which introduces Part 1 of Schedule 17A) for "and the PRA" substitute ", and between the FCA and the PRA,".

44 In section 345A (PRA disciplinary measures) omit subsection (6).

45 (1) Section 348 (restrictions on disclosure of confidential information) is amended as follows.

(2) In subsection (5)(aa) for "PRA" substitute "Bank of England".

(3) At the end insert—

"(8) In this section references to the Bank of England include the Bank acting in its capacity as the PRA."

46 (1) Section 353A (restriction on disclosing information received from Bank) is amended as follows.

(2) In subsection (1) for "A regulator" substitute "The FCA".

(3) In subsection (3) for the words from "the regulator" to the end substitute "the FCA received the information from the Bank of England."

(4) In subsection (4) for "regulator to which it disclosed the information" substitute "FCA".

(5) In subsection (6)—

(a) omit paragraph (a);

(b) in paragraph (d) for "regulator" substitute "FCA".

(6) In subsection (7)—

(a) in the words before paragraph (a) for "a regulator" substitute "the FCA";

(b) in paragraphs (a)(i) and (b) for "regulator" substitute "FCA".

(7) In subsection (8)—

(a) for "a regulator" substitute "the FCA";

(b) for "that regulator" substitute "the FCA".

(8) In subsection (9)—

(a) for "Each regulator" substitute "The FCA";

(b) in paragraphs (b) and (c) for "regulator" substitute "FCA".

(9) After subsection (9) insert—

"(10) In this section references to the Bank of England include the Bank acting in its capacity as the PRA."

47 In section 354B(2) (PRA's duty to co-operate) for the words from "Bank" to the end substitute "FCA (but see section 3D)".

48 Omit section 354C (PRA's general duty to provide information to Bank).

49 In section 417(1) (definitions) after the definition of "authorised person" insert—

> ""Bank of England" is to be read in accordance with section 2A(4) to (6);".

50 (1) Schedule 1ZB (Prudential Regulation Authority) is amended as follows.

(2) In the shoulder note, for "2A" substitute "2AB."

(3) In paragraph 1—

(a) omit the definition of "the Bank";

(b) for "2A(6)" substitute "2AB(3)".

(4) Omit paragraphs 2 to 16 and 18.

(5) In paragraph 19 (annual report)—

(a) in sub-paragraph (1), in the words before paragraph (a), for "Treasury" substitute "Chancellor of the Exchequer";

(b) omit sub-paragraph (3)(a);

(c) in sub-paragraph (4)—

(i) for "Treasury" substitute "Chancellor of the Exchequer";

(ii) for "them" substitute "the Chancellor";

(d) after sub-paragraph (4) insert—

> "(5) The Chancellor may comply with sub-paragraph (4) by laying a document containing a report under this paragraph together with a report under section 4 of the Bank of England Act 1998."

(6) Omit paragraphs 22 to 26.

(7) In paragraph 31—

(a) in sub-paragraph (2) for "2A(6)" substitute "2AB(3)";

(b) in sub-paragraph (4) for "2A(6)(d)" substitute "2AB(3)(d)".

51 (1) Schedule 17A (exercise of Part 18 functions by Bank of England) is amended as follows.

(2) In paragraph 2(1) for "appropriate regulators" substitute "FCA".

(3) In paragraph 17—

(a) in sub-paragraph (5), for the words from "the reference" to the end substitute "subsection (1)(a) required consultation with the FCA.";

(b) omit sub-paragraph (6)(b).

(4) In paragraph 23—

(a) the existing text becomes sub-paragraph (1);

(b) after that sub-paragraph insert—

> "(2) Paragraph 9(2)(a) does not apply to the reference to the PRA in section 348(8)."

(5) In paragraph 35(3)—

(a) at the end of paragraph (a) insert "and";

(b) omit paragraph (b).

Banking Act 2009 (c. 1)

52 The Banking Act 2009 is amended as follows.

53 In section 83ZZ (co-operation)—

(a) at the end of paragraph (a) insert ", and";

(b) omit paragraph (b).

54 (1) Section 83Z1 (delegation of enforcement functions) is amended as follows.

(2) In subsection (1)—

(a) for "appropriate regulator" substitute "FCA";

(b) for "that regulator" substitute "the FCA".

(3) Omit subsection (2)(b).

(4) In subsection (3), for "appropriate regulator" substitute "FCA".

55 In section 89L(2)(c)(i) (application of section 348 of Financial Services and Markets Act 2000) omit inserted paragraph (ca).

56 (1) Section 96 (ground for applying for bank insolvency order) is amended as follows.

(2) In subsection (2)(a) omit "the PRA has informed the Bank of England that".

(3) In subsection (3)(a), for the words from "has", in the first place it occurs, to the end substitute "is satisfied that Condition 2 in section 7 is met, and".

57 (1) Section 108 (removal of bank liquidator by court) is amended as follows.

(2) In subsection (2) omit "the Bank of England and".

(3) In subsection (3) omit "the PRA and".

58 In section 117(2)(a) (consents required for making of bank insolvency order) omit "the Bank of England and".

59 (1) In section 129A (modifications for banks not regulated by PRA), the table in subsection (2) is amended as follows.

(2) In the entry for section 96, in column 2, for paragraphs (a) and (b) substitute—

"(a) Read subsection (2)(a) as "the FCA has informed the Bank of England that the FCA is satisfied that Condition 1 in section 7 is met,".

(b) Treat the references to the PRA in subsection (3) as references to the FCA.

(ba) Read subsection (3)(a) as "the Bank of England—(i) has informed the FCA that it is satisfied that Condition 2 in section 7 is met, and (ii) has consented to the application,"."

(3) In the entry for section 108, in column 2—

(a) for paragraph (b) substitute—

"(b) Treat the reference in subsection (2) to the FCA as a reference to the Bank of England.";

(b) omit paragraph (c).

(4) In the entry for section 117, in column 2, for paragraph (b) substitute—

"(b) Treat the reference in subsection (2) to the FCA as a reference to the Bank of England."

60 Omit section 204(4)(ba) (Bank may disclose information to PRA).

61 Omit section 246(2)(b) (Bank may disclose information to PRA).

62 Before section 257 insert—

"256B Bank of England" and "Prudential Regulation Authority"

"256B Bank of England" and "Prudential Regulation Authority"

(1) In this Act references to the Bank of England do not include the Bank acting in its capacity as the Prudential Regulation Authority.

(2) For the interpretation of references to the Prudential Regulation Authority, see section 2A of the Financial Services and Markets Act 2000."

63 In section 261 (index of defined terms), at the appropriate places in the table insert—

"Bank of England	256B"
"Prudential Regulation Authority	256B"

Financial Services Act 2012 (c. 21)

64 The Financial Services Act 2012 is amended as follows.

65 In section 85(8) (definition of relevant functions) for "2A(6)" substitute "2AB(3)".

66 (1) Section 117 (interpretation) is amended as follows.

(2) In subsection (2), in the definition of "the PRA", at the end insert "(and see section 2A of the Financial Services and Markets Act 2000 for the interpretation of references to the Prudential Regulation Authority)".

(3) After subsection (2) insert—

"(2A) In this Act references to the Bank of England do not include the Bank acting in its capacity as the PRA."

Financial Services (Banking Reform) Act 2013 (c. 33)

67 In section 98(5)(d) of the Financial Services (Banking Reform) Act 2013 (definition of relevant functions), for "2A(6)" substitute "2AB(3)".

Repeals

68 The following provisions are repealed.

Short title and chapter	*Extent of repeal*
Banking Act 2009 (c. 1)	Section 238(2).
Financial Services Act 2012 (c. 21)	Section 2(3).

Short title and chapter	*Extent of repeal*
Financial Services (Banking Reform) Act 2013 (c. 33)	Section 3(3), (4)(a), (4)(b)(i) and (4)(d). In Schedule 2, paragraphs 1(13) and 2(7). In Schedule 3, paragraph 17.

SCHEDULE 3

Section 17

SAVING AND TRANSITIONAL PROVISION RELATING TO PART 1

Interpretation

1 In this Schedule—

"the Bank" means the Bank of England;

"the company" means the body corporate originally incorporated as the Prudential Regulation Authority Limited and renamed as the Prudential Regulation Authority by section 2A of the Financial Services and Markets Act 2000 (as it had effect before section 12 came into force);

"enactment" has the same meaning as in Part 1A of that Act (see section 3T);

"transferred function" means a function transferred from the company to the Bank by virtue of section 12;

"transferred property" means any property, right or liability transferred from the company to the Bank by virtue of section 15.

Saving for orders under section 2A(6)(d) of the Financial Services and Markets Act 2000

2 An order made under section 2A(6)(d) of the Financial Services and Markets Act 2000 before section 12 of this Act comes into force—

(a) is not revoked by virtue of section 12 coming into force, and

(b) may be amended or revoked as if made under section 2AB(3)(d) of the Financial Services and Markets Act 2000 (inserted by section 12).

Prudential regulation strategy

3 (1) Sub-paragraph (2) applies to the strategy determined by the company under section 2E of the Financial Services and Markets Act 2000 which is in effect immediately before section 12 comes into force.

(2) After section 12 comes into force the strategy is to continue to have effect, and is to be treated as having been determined under section 2E of that Act by the Bank in its capacity as the Prudential Regulation Authority.

Prudential regulation budget

4 (1) Sub-paragraph (2) applies to the budget adopted by the company under paragraph 18 of Schedule 1ZB to the Financial Services and Markets Act 2000 for the financial year in which section 12 comes into force.

(2) After section 12 comes into force the budget is to be treated as the budget for the Bank's functions as the Prudential Regulation Authority for the financial year to which it relates, adopted by the Prudential Regulation Committee of the Bank under paragraph 18 of Schedule 6A to the Bank of England Act 1998.

Annual report

5 (1) Sub-paragraphs (2) and (3) apply to the first report under paragraph 19 of Schedule 1ZB to the Financial Services and Markets Act 2000 made by the Bank in its capacity as the Prudential Regulation Authority.

(2) The report must be made not later than a year after the last report made under that paragraph by the company.

(3) If section 12 came into force during the period to which the report relates ("the reporting period"), the report must deal with things done by the company during the reporting period before that section came into force (as well as things done by the Bank in its capacity as the Prudential Regulation Authority after that section came into force).

Information

6 (1) The company may disclose to the Bank any information which the company considers that it is necessary or expedient to disclose to the Bank in preparation for the commencement of section 12.

(2) Section 348 of the Financial Services and Markets Act 2000 (restrictions on disclosure of confidential information) has effect subject to sub-paragraph (1).

Corporation tax: intangible assets

7 (1) This paragraph applies for the purposes of Part 8 of the Corporation Tax Act 2009.

(2) Expressions used in this paragraph have the same meaning as in that Part.

(3) The transfer of a chargeable intangible asset is a tax-neutral transfer.

(4) An intangible fixed asset which is a pre-FA 2002 asset of the company at the time of the transfer is to be treated, on and after the transfer, as a pre-FA 2002 asset of the Bank.

(5) "Transfer" means a transfer from the company to the Bank by virtue of section 15.

Construction of enactments

8 (1) Section 2A(1) and (3) of the Financial Services and Markets Act 2000 (meaning of "Prudential Regulation Authority") does not apply to an enactment if and to the extent that the enactment makes provision about a time before section 12 came into force.

(2) In relation to such a time references to the Prudential Regulation Authority are to the company.

Construction of other documents

9 (1) Sub-paragraph (2) applies to any provision in a document other than an enactment that—

(a) relates to a transferred function and is in effect immediately before the function is transferred, or

(b) relates to transferred property and is in effect immediately before the property is transferred.

(2) After the function or the property is transferred, any references in the provision (however expressed)—

(a) to or including the company, or

(b) having effect as references to or including the company,

are to be read, so far as is appropriate in consequence of the transfer, as to or including the Bank in its capacity as the Prudential Regulation Authority.

Continuity: general provision

10 (1) The transfer of functions from the company to the Bank by virtue of section 12 does not affect the validity of anything done (or having effect as if done) by or in relation to the company before that section comes into force.

(2) The transfer of property, rights and liabilities from the company to the Bank by virtue of section 15 does not affect the validity of anything done (or having effect as if done) by or in relation to the company before that section comes into force.

11 (1) Sub-paragraph (2) applies to anything that—

(a) is done (or has effect as if done) by or in relation to the company for the purposes of, or otherwise in connection with, a transferred function or transferred property, and

(b) is in effect immediately before the function or property is transferred.

(2) Anything to which this sub-paragraph applies is to be treated, so far as is appropriate in consequence of the transfer, as done by or in relation to the Bank, in its capacity as the Prudential Regulation Authority.

12 There may be continued by or in relation to the Bank, in its capacity as the Prudential Regulation Authority, anything (including legal proceedings) that—

(a) relates to a transferred function or transferred property, and

(b) is in the process of being done by or in relation to the company immediately before the function or property is transferred.

SCHEDULE 4

Section 21

EXTENSION OF RELEVANT AUTHORISED PERSONS REGIME TO ALL AUTHORISED PERSONS

Amendments of Financial Services and Markets Act 2000

1 The Financial Services and Markets Act 2000 is amended as follows.

2 (1) Section 59 (approval for particular arrangements) is amended as follows.

(2) For subsection (6A) substitute—

"(6A) If the FCA is satisfied that a function of a description specified in rules made by the FCA under subsection (3)(a) or (b) is a senior management function as defined in section 59ZA, the FCA must designate the function in the rules as a senior management function."

(3) Omit subsections (6B) and (6C).

3 After section 59ZA insert—

"59ZB Designated senior management functions

"59ZB Designated senior management functions

For the purposes of this Part the following are "designated senior management functions"—

(a) a function of a description specified in rules made by the FCA under section 59(3)(a) or (b) which is designated as a senior management function by the FCA under section 59(6A);

(b) a function of a description specified in rules made by the PRA under section 59(3)(a)."

4 (1) Section 60 (applications for approval) is amended as follows.

(2) In subsection (2A), omit—

(a) the "and" at the end of paragraph (a);

(b) paragraph (b).

(3) Omit subsection (2C).

(4) Omit subsection (6A).

5 (1) Section 60A (vetting of candidates by relevant authorised persons) is amended as follows.

(2) In the heading omit "relevant".

(3) In subsection (1) for "a relevant" substitute "an".

(4) Omit subsection (3).

6 (1) Section 61 (determination of applications) is amended as follows.

(2) In subsection (1)(b), omit from "in relation" to ""relevant senior" and insert "(a "senior".

(3) In subsections (2B) and (3ZA) omit "relevant".

(4) Omit subsections (6) and (7).

7 In section 62A(4) (changes in responsibilities of senior managers - definitions) omit the definition of "designated senior management function".

8 In section 63(2A) (authorised person's duty to review approvals)—

(a) omit "relevant" in the first place it occurs;

(b) omit the words after paragraph (b).

9 In the heading of section 63ZA (variation of senior manager's approval at request of relevant authorised person) omit "relevant".

10 (1) Section 63ZB (variation of senior manager's approval on initiative of regulator) is amended as follows.

(2) In subsection (1), for "a relevant" substitute "an".

(3) In subsection (2)—

(a) for "a relevant" substitute "an";

(b) in paragraph (a)(ii) omit "relevant".

(4) Omit subsections (5) and (6).

11 (1) Section 63E (certification of employees by relevant authorised persons) is amended as follows.

(2) In the heading omit "relevant".

(3) In subsection (1), for "A relevant" substitute "An".

(4) In subsection (3) for "a relevant", in each place it occurs, substitute "an".

(5) In subsection (4) omit "relevant" in each place it occurs.

(6) In subsection (6)(b) omit "relevant".

(7) In subsection (8) omit the definition of "relevant PRA-authorised person".

(8) Omit subsection (10).

12 (1) Section 63F (issuing of certificates) is amended as follows.

(2) In subsection (1) for "A relevant" substitute "An".

(3) In subsection (2) omit "relevant".

(4) In subsection (4) for "a relevant" substitute "an".

(5) In subsection (6) for "a relevant" substitute "an".

(6) In subsection (7) for "A relevant" substitute "An".

13 (1) Section 64A (rules of conduct) is amended as follows.

(2) In subsection (1)(b), for the words from "relevant" to the end substitute "authorised persons".

(3) In subsection (2)(c) omit "relevant".

(4) In subsection (3) omit the definition of "relevant PRA-authorised person".

14 (1) Section 64B (conduct rules) is amended as follows.

(2) In the heading omit "relevant".

(3) In subsection (2) omit "relevant" in the first place it occurs.

(4) In subsection (3) for "a relevant" substitute "an".

(5) Omit subsection (7).

15 (1) Section 64C (requirement to notify regulator of disciplinary action) is amended as follows.

(2) In the heading omit "relevant".

(3) In subsection (1)—

(a) in paragraph (a) for "a relevant", in the first place it occurs, substitute "an";

(b) in the words after paragraph (b) omit "relevant".

(4) In subsection (3)—

(a) in paragraph (a) omit "relevant authorised persons that are";

(b) in paragraph (b) omit "relevant".

(5) Omit subsection (5).

16 (1) Section 66A (misconduct: action by FCA) is amended as follows.

(2) In subsection (2)(b)(ii) for "a relevant" substitute "an".

(3) In subsection (3)(b)(ii) omit "in the case of a relevant authorised person,".

(4) In subsection (5)(a) for "a relevant" substitute "an".

(5) In subsection (7)—

(a) in the definition of "senior manager", for "a relevant" substitute "an";

(b) omit the definition of "designated senior management function".

(6) Omit subsection (9).

17 (1) Section 66B (misconduct: action by PRA) is amended as follows.

(2) In subsection (2)(b)(ii) omit "relevant".

(3) In subsection (3)(b), for sub-paragraph (ii) substitute—

"(ii) an employee of the PRA-authorised person".

(4) In subsection (5)(a) omit "relevant".

(5) In subsection (7)—

(a) in the definition of "senior manager", omit "relevant";

(b) omit the definition of "designated senior management function".

(6) In subsection (8) omit the definition of "relevant PRA-authorised person".

(7) Omit subsection (9).

18 Omit section 71A (meaning of "relevant authorised person").

19 (1) Section 347 (record of authorised persons etc) is amended as follows.

(2) In subsection (2)—

(a) in paragraph (g)(iv), omit "in a case where the authorised person concerned is a relevant authorised person,";

(b) in paragraph (h) for "a relevant" substitute "an".

(3) In subsection (8A)—

(a) omit the definition of "relevant authorised person";

(b) in the definition of "senior manager", for "a relevant" substitute "an";

(c) in the definition of "designated senior management function", for the words from "means" to the end substitute "has the meaning given by section 59ZB."

20 In section 415B(5) (consultation in relation to enforcement action), in the definition of "relevant senior management function", for the words from "has been" to the end substitute "is a designated senior management function as defined by section 59ZB)."

21 In section 429(1)(a) (orders subject to affirmative resolution procedure) omit "71A(4),".

Consequential amendments of Financial Services (Banking Reform) Act 2013

22 (1) The Financial Services (Banking Reform) Act 2013 is amended as follows.

(2) Omit section 18(4) (which inserts the subsections substituted or omitted by paragraph 2).

(3) Omit section 20(3) (which inserts the subsection omitted by paragraph 4(4)).

(4) Omit section 23(6) (which inserts the subsections omitted by paragraph 6(4)).

(5) Omit section 33 (which inserts the section omitted by paragraph 18).

(6) For section 37(8) (interpretation) substitute—

"(8) Senior management function" means—

(a) a function of a description specified in rules made by the FCA under section 59(3)(a) or (b) of FSMA 2000 which is designated as a senior management function by the FCA under section 59(6A) of that Act;

(b) a function of a description specified in rules made by the PRA under section 59(3)(a) of that Act."

(7) Omit section 136(2)(a) (which inserts the words omitted by paragraph 21).

GRANGIS - UK PUBLISHING 2022.

www.ingramcontent.com/pod-product-compliance
Lightning Source LLC
LaVergne TN
LVHW060214210926
848481LV00008B/2733